A Compendium of Essays:

Purcell, Hogarth and Handel, Beethoven, Liszt, Debussy, and Andrew Lloyd Webber

E. A. Bucchianeri

Batalha Publishers
Maxieira, Portugal

Hardback, Second Edition 2010
ISBN: 978-989-96844-2-3

Library of Congress Subject Headings

Bucchianeri, E.A.
A Compedium of Essays: Purcell, Hogarth and Handel, Beethoven, Liszt, Debussy,and Andrew Lloyd Webber
Bibliography
Includes Index
1. Classical music.   2. Beethoven, Ludwig van, 1770-1827 Appreciation.   3. Beethoven, Ludwig van, 1770-1827. Symphonies--Criticism and interpretation.   4. Debussy, Claude, 1862-1918.   5. Debussy, Claude, 1862-1918--Criticism and interpretation. 6. Handel, George Frideric, 1685-1759—Influence. 7. Handel, George Frideric, 1685-1759—Portraits.   8. Hogarth, William, 1697-1764--Criticism and interpretation.   9. Hogarth, William, 1697-1764. Rake's progress.   10. Liszt, Franz, 1811-1886--Criticism and interpretation.   11. Liszt, Franz, 1811-1886. Faust symphony.   12. Liszt, Franz, 1811-1886. Symphonic poems.   13. Lloyd Webber, Andrew, 1948- Phantom of the Opera.   14. Orchestral music--Analysis, appreciation. 15. Popular music and classical music. 16. Purcell, Henry, 1659-1695. Dido & Aeneas

British Library Subject Headings

Bucchianeri, E.A.
A Compendium of Essays: Purcell, Hogarth and Handel, Beethoven, Liszt, Debussy, and Andrew Lloyd Webber
1. Beethoven, Ludwig van, 1770-1827—Symphonies.   2. Composers.   3. Debussy, Claude, 1862-1918.   4. Handel, George Frideric, 1685-1759.   5. Hogarth, William, 1687-1764, Rake's Progress.   6. Liszt, Franz, 1811-1886—Symphonic Poems.   7. Musical Play in English, Lloyd Webber, Andrew, 1948-.   8. Music.   9. Phantom of the Opera (Musical).   10. Purcell, Henry, 1659-1695-- Dido and Aeneas

"The fire which seems out
often sleeps beneath the cinders."

Pierre Corneille

Books by the same Author

Handel's Path to Covent Garden

Faust: My Soul be Damned for the World

Table of Contents

Acknowledgments:

I sincerely wish to thank Lord Andrew Lloyd Webber, his publicist Daniel Bee of Brown Lloyd James Ltd., and the Really Useful Group for graciously granting me permission to study the scores of *The Phantom of the Opera*. I also extend my sincere gratitude Caroline Skidmore and the staff at R.U.G. for their kindness and their help during my research in their office when they were overwhelmingly busy.

My heartfelt appreciation to Ben Duncan and Jeremy Smith of the Guildhall Library who assisted with the illustrations featuring William Hogarth's engravings "The Rake's Levée" (1735) and "The Enraged Musician" (1741): reproduced by kind permission of the Guildhall Library, Corporation of London.

෨•෨

Purcell's *Dido and Aeneas:*
A Musical Exemplum for Young Gentlewomen

Henry Purcell's opera *Dido and Aeneas* (1689) has intrigued and fascinated many musicologists and music lovers through the years. This is the only opera he composed with a musical score that contains no spoken dialogue in contrast to his semi-operas, and to this day, is considered one of the finest examples of English Baroque opera. Composed for the young ladies of an elite Chelsea boarding school, it fell into obscurity after its premiere and did not resurface again until 1700, revived to fit an adaptation of Shakespeare's play *Measure for Measure.*[1] According to the *Oxford Companion to Music,* the original opera did not appear in a restored form for the stage until 1895.[2] Why did producers overlook *Dido and Aeneas* for so long?

Curtis Price offers some possible explanations concerning this operatic oversight in his introduction to the *Norton Critical Score* edition. He suggests it may have been suppressed as contemporary London audiences could have objected to opera featuring continuous singing, and he also proposes Purcell possibly suppressed his own work due to its experimental form.[3] Price surmises the political

---

[1] Curtis Price, ed., *A Norton Critical Score, Henry Purcell, Dido and Aeneas, An Opera* (New York: W.W. Norton and Company, 1986), p. ix.

[2] Percy A. Scholes, *The Oxford Companion to Music* (Oxford: Oxford University Press, 1943), p. 62.

[3] *Norton Score,* ibid.

implication connected with the libretto, written by Nahum Tate, is the most obvious cause for its apparent suppression from the operatic stage. He recalls the arguments of John Buttrey who stated that many of the major English operatic works during 1656–1695 were specifically composed to praise the monarchy if not the monarch.[4] According to Price's observations, the subject of *Dido and Aeneas* derived from Virgil's classic *Aeneid* contained unflattering connotations to the reigning monarchs, William and Mary (1689–95). In the original tale, Aeneas of Troy has set sail for Italy; his destiny is to establish a new nation, however, his ships, blown off course by a tempest, arrive at an African port and he receives a hospitable welcome from the Carthaginians. Queen Dido, enamoured by his tales of adventure, falls in love and plans to marry him. During a hunting entertainment, an approaching storm forces them to seek shelter in a cave where they have an illicit affair. Subsequently, Jupiter dispatches Mercury to Aeneas who warns him to continue his journey and leave Carthage. He prepares for his voyage secretly without informing Queen Dido, who nevertheless discovers his deceit. He ignores her pleadings to remain with her and she suffers a tragic death by her own hand. Price remarks, "The story of a prince who seduces and abandons a neurotic queen would seem a tactless way to honor the new monarchs."[5]

Price maintains these unfortunate associations were the main cause for Tate's criticised censorship of the plot.

---

[4] Ibid. pp. 6–7.
[5] Ibid. p. 6.

"... Tate was forced to adapt the classical tale, already deeply entwined with the supposed origins of the British monarchy, to disengage Queen Mary from a symbolic link with Queen Dido. This required major changes of plot, motivation, and characterisation. I believe that the gaping ambiguities in the libretto — the reason for Dido's grief in Act I, the uncertain consummation of the couple's love in Act II, the enchantresses' unmotivated hatred of the queen, and even the manner of Dido's death — are owing directly to the potentially sensitive nature of the allegory. Had Tate followed Virgil as closely as in *Brutus of Alba*, faithfully depicting the queen's obsessive love for Aeneas, their winter of debauchery, her paralysing guilt, extreme bitterness, and blazing anger at his departure, eyebrows would have been raised from Chelsea to Whitehall."[6]

It is possible this allegorical association, despite the censorship of the original drama, was a leading factor in the suppression of this opera. Virgil's classic would have been familiar to audiences of the day and the unfortunate associations with the plot would still hold true. Purcell was wise not to have this work produced more than once; it may have been construed as an insult to the reigning monarchs regardless of the alterations Tate made to the original epic.

---

[6] Ibid. pp. 8–9.

11

However, this association may not be the only reason the opera's revival did not take place much sooner in its original form, nor does it fully explain the ambiguities and the alterations of the plot and characterisation. We may consider these allegorical references a *secondary reason* for the opera's descent into near oblivion. Upon reading the various historical essays and contributions concerning *Dido and Aeneas* contained within the *Norton Critical Score* edition, I was quite surprised to find not one featured a commentary on the epilogue written by Thomas Durfey that was recited at the premiere:

The Epilogue

All that we know the angels do above,
I've read, is that they sing and that they love,
The vocal part we have tonight perform'd
And if by Love our hearts are not yet warm'd
Great Providence has still more bounteous been
To save us from these grand deceivers, men.
Here blest with innocence, and peace of mind,
Not only bred to virtue, but inclin'd;
We flourish, and defy all human kind.
Art's curious garden thus we learn to know,
And here secure from nipping blasts we grow,
Let the vain fop range o'er yon vile lewd town,
Learn play-house wit, and vow 'tis all his own;
Let him cock, huff, strut, ogle, lie, and swear
How he's admired by such and such a player;

All's one to us, his charms have here no power;

Our hearts have just the temper as before;

Besides, to show we live with strictest rules,

Our nunnery-door is charm'd to shut out fools;

No love-toy here can pass to private view,

Nor China orange cramm'd with billet doux,

Rome may allow strange tricks to please her sons,

But we are Protestants and English nuns;

Like nimble fawns, and birds that bless the spring

Unscarr'd by turning times we dance and sing;

We hope to please, but if some critic here

Fond of wit, designs to be severe,

Let not his patience be worn out too soon;

In a few years we shall all be in tune.[7]

This epilogue may be the key to unlock the mysteries concerning *Dido and Aeneas*, our main observation centres on its subject and nature. The epilogue is not a conclusion or a summary of the story of *Dido and Aeneas* per se, but a description of the students of the Chelsea boarding school and the moral values the school wished to uphold. Presented as a safe environment secluded from the outside world, the school offers a place of sanctuary where the pupils may study in peace and develop a standard of high moral values. It would appear this epilogue reveals the intended purpose of the opera, i.e. it was a work to enhance the moral edification of the students. Notice the amusing sixth and seventh lines describing men

---

[7] Ibid. p.76. The Epilogue first appeared in Durfey's *New Poems* (1689): "Epilogue to the Opera of Dido and Aeneas, perform'd at Mr. Preist's Boarding School at Chelsea; Spoken by the Lady Dorothy Burk."

as 'grand deceivers' — does this imply a warning to the young ladies? In addition, could it be possible that *Dido and Aeneas* was intended as an open-day entertainment for the relatives of the young students? The opera premiered in the spring; A. Margaret Laurie suggests Purcell composed it for the coronation of William and Mary on April 11, 1689.[8] This would have been an ideal occasion to hold an open day for families of the attending students, allowing them to celebrate the festivities together. The epilogue not only presents a reminder of school values to the students, but also exhibits a public relations tactic by using rhetoric that would reassure any parent their children were acquiring the correct principles expected from a prestigious institution. Furthermore, when Purcell composed *Dido and Aeneas* he considered the musical capabilities of the young ladies, and this would have provided an opportunity for the students to display their musical accomplishments to their relatives. This may also explain why this work is Purcell's only all-sung opera; young students have been traditionally recognised as the promoters of radical ideas — the students of the Chelsea school may have favoured a more innovative style and could have requested a work which was different from the traditional genres in vogue at that time. Notice the last four lines of the epilogue; they beg critics in the audience to excuse any faults with their performance through lack of experience. The mention of possible critics may also signify the presence of outsiders who would not normally be present at the school.

Therefore, this epilogue apparently indicates *Dido and Aeneas* was a special commission for the boarding school for a

---

[8] A. Margaret Laurie, 'Allegory, Sources, and Early Performance History', *Norton Score*, p. 45.

specific occasion and Purcell was not anticipating a future public performance. In addition, it explains Tate's censorship of Virgil's original classic in his libretto. If the intended design of the opera was to present a morally edifying entertainment, we are not surprised they excluded the illicit details. What parent would want their young daughter subjected to a work promoting debauchery and suicide? Let us examine how they edited and modified the plot to suit this specific occasion.

According to the *Aeneid*, Dido is grieving for her dead husband Sychaeus.[9] In contrast, there is no evidence in Tate's libretto that Dido was a widow and therefore he does not remain true to Virgil's original character. In the libretto, the cause of her sorrow is not this misfortune and it would have been a simple matter to include this small detail; there is no mention of Sychaeus, and apparently, they intended this omission. The cause of Dido's grief originates from her conflicting emotions concerning Aeneas. Belinda, Dido's confidante, discerns this fact and voices her observation, "Then let me speak, the Trojan guest, / into your tender thoughts has pressed." One of Dido's fears is also expressed by Belinda's following lines and by one of the ladies of the court, "Fear no danger to ensue / The hero loves as well as you." Apparently, Dido's sorrow originates with the possibility her love would remain unrequited, yet, her fears have a deeper foundation, she knows his fate lies elsewhere despite her own desires as observed in Belinda's first line of Act I, "Shake the cloud from off your brow, / Fate your wishes does allow." Therefore, Sychaeus is not included in the drama and as a result Dido's character has been changed; she is not a

---

[9] *Norton Score*, p. 12.

15

grieving widow, but a maiden queen. I theorise this was a tactic designed to create an empathic association between the young ladies and Dido. The epilogue refers to the students as 'English nuns' and compares the school to a 'nunnery' with a 'door charm'd to shut out fools'. This is one instance where they apparently changed the plot to accommodate the cast and audience, further supporting the conjecture they composed the opera exclusively for the Chelsea school.

Other plot alterations can be easily explained when viewed in this light. For instance, it would be scandalous to have the love affair between Dido and Aeneas referred to in the school production, as this would contradict the moral policies of the establishment mentioned in the epilogue. If we examine the time sequence presented in Acts I and II, we will observe that the affair could not have taken place; apparently, they avoided leaving the incident open to the imagination if at all possible. In Act I, we can observe that Dido and Aeneas have not yet professed their love to each other before departing on the hunt. Dido in Act I also strives to discourage him, for in her last line she retorts, "Fate forbids what you pursue." It appears she is attempting to remain emotionally detached from Aeneas despite her feelings for him as Belinda says to Aeneas, "Pursue thy conquest, Love – her Eyes / Confess the flame her tongue denies." The concluding chorus of Act I suggests they have left for the hunting expedition, "To the hills and the vales, to the rocks and the / mountains ...." In Act II we are presented with the scheming witches; the Sorceress has planned to destroy the queen and proclaims the coven will have Dido ruined before the day ends, "Ere sunset shall most wretched prove / Deprived of fame, life and love."

Notice also the Sorceress relates Dido and Aeneas are on the hunting expedition at that same moment, "The Queen and he are now in chase, / Hark, how the cry comes on apace." This information confirms that on the same day Dido and Aeneas have not requited their love before they leave on the hunting expedition, and are doomed to part before sunset. It is possible the Sorceress' lines regarding the hunt could also imply a growing love affair, yet, according to the stage direction when the scene changes to the outdoor expedition, we know they were never alone; the court entourage accompany them at all times and they are entertained by dancers. In addition, the storm the witches brew does not drive them to seek the shelter of a cave as in the *Aeneid*, it merely causes Dido and the court to flee to the town while Aeneas is left behind to receive the message from Mercury's impostor sent by the Sorceress. Apparently, their romance never progressed beyond the stages of 'blushing' and the 'admission of feelings'. Under these circumstances, how can a passionate affair suddenly blossom within this short space of time? Furthermore, Aeneas' line "One night enjoyed, the next forsook" is merely poetic when considering they had only professed their love for each other that day; there is no time allocated for the previous night.

Evidently, they altered the plot to accommodate the intended audience; they omitted illicit scenes, and they characterised Dido as a maiden queen determined in the beginning not to fall prey to the follies of an idealised romance. She is reluctant to admit her feelings and resists his first entreaties — she remains steadfast until finally, duped by his suave persuasions, she promises to love him in return. Apparently, the message conveyed by her actions was to portray romance as a serious issue, and should be avoided at all cost with respect to the age of the students. Notice these lines from the epilogue, "And if by Love our hearts are not yet warm'd / Great Providence has still more bounteous been … ." Possibly, Dido's character was developed to exemplify the consequences when prudence is ignored and reality is 'numbed' by the prospect of idealised love; she is a classic illustration of self-persuasion backfiring as Aeneas apparently points out in his lines "No sooner she resigns her heart, / But from her arms I'm forced to part." Here he indicates that he has betrayed Dido's love, we must remember an illicit affair has not occurred and the actual presentation of their brief relationship is depicted as an exemplum; the plot may have been constructed in this fashion to support a moral undertone for the young ladies who may be allured by an idealised view of romance. The intention of this allegory may have been to discourage the girls from succumbing to a worldly romance, thus diverting their path of virtue, which may ultimately lead to dire consequences.

On further inspection, it is interesting to note the structure of the opera seems to pivot on the concept of making decisions and the ultimate possibility of hazardous results. Act I symbolises the procedure in making a decision; Dido contemplates succumbing to her emotions to love Aeneas although she is already aware his destiny lies elsewhere. She ponders on her judgement, takes counsel from her courtiers, and finally she considers the entreaties of Aeneas who promises he will "defy / The feeble stroke of Destiny." Act II demonstrates the enactment of the decisions made; Dido and Aeneas take part in the celebratory hunting entertainment, each anticipating the prospect of a future happy union. The Sorceress and her "wayward sisters" are introduced to us in Act II, informing us of the mischief she intends; they execute the diabolical plan to destroy Dido and Carthage already decided upon by the Sorceress. Act III exhibits the repercussions of the decisions determined in Act I and effected in Act II; Dido's fear of Aeneas departing in quest of his destiny shown in Act I materialises to haunt her. She unexpectedly discovers that he is making preparations for his departure without informing her, and she realises his promise was empty and meaningless; she is compelled to face the prospect that he intended to abscond without notice:

> No repentance shall reclaim
> The injured Dido's slighted flame.
> For 'tis enough whate'er you now decree,
> That you had once a thought of leaving me.

Aeneas enters the scene; a confrontation ensues between the two characters and she dismisses his sanctimonious and hypocritical excuses. Having perceived his paltry character, she orders him to depart and he exits. The realisation that she had succumbed to his false and empty promises combined with her own unrealistic idealism of love divides her emotionally; she cannot live with the knowledge of Aeneas' true character, yet she yearns for his faithless love. She is ultimately doomed to die of a broken heart and she embraces her approaching death:

> Away!
> To death I'll fly, if longer you delay.

But death, alas, I cannot shun,
Death must come when he is gone. …

Thy hand Belinda, darkness shades me,
On thy bosom let me rest.
More I would but death invades me.
Death is now a welcome guest.

Purcell's predominant key structure within the opera, i.e. C minor to G minor, seems to reflect this decision-making process which culminates with devastating results. The overture commences in C minor; apparently, the key of Dido's first portrayal of grief concerning Aeneas as observed in her first aria. The aria begins in C minor with the text, "Ah! Belinda I am press'd, / With torment not to be confess'd. / Peace and I are strangers grown," and modulates to G minor on the words "I languish till my grief is known." The key returns to C minor for the conclusion of the aria. In Act III, when Dido is resigned to her fate, the recitative preceding her famous lament "When I am laid in Earth" mirrors this key relationship; the recitative beginning in C minor, "Thy hand Belinda …" and concluding with the famous ground bass in G minor of Dido's lament. The finale ends in the key of G minor; a symbolic arrangement exhibiting the realisation of her apprehensions presented in Act I.

Returning to our examination of the plot alterations, let us concentrate on the treatment of Aeneas' character. In general, they presented Aeneas as a disloyal, selfish and deceitful person. Often, he is regarded as a minor character, for his part in relation to the opera is small, however, his role within the drama is larger than life; he is more than a 'complete booby' as Joseph Kerman[10] describes him! He is the catalyst for the tragedy and possesses all the hallmarks of a 'grand deceiver' as the epilogue stereotyped men. In the first Act, Aeneas promises Dido he will defy the gods as a declaration of his love for her, however, when he receives the message from Mercury's impostor to depart, he readily submits to the command and proceeds with preparations to leave disregarding his oath to the queen. Robert Savage[11] maintains this could actually be a pious trait as there is no evidence to suspect the message was delivered by a false Mercury, yet, Dido immediately recognises Aeneas' sanctimonious deceit, "Thus hypocrites that murder act / Make heaven and gods the authors of the fact." In addition, one must consider the sequence of his reactions; it may be commendable that he wishes to conform to the god's commands, but it also displays his primary intentions. He did not consider how this decree would affect the queen for his first reply centres on his preparations to sail. When he eventually reflects on how Dido may react to this decision, his choice of words is interesting, "But ah! What language can I try, / My injured Queen to pacify?" He has literally stated with the word 'pacify'— "how do I tell her and get off the hook?" Next, he deflects the blame to the gods whom he believes have sent the message, "Yours be the blame, ye gods, for I / Obey your will ...." We may dispense with his so-called commendable piety! Furthermore, if this message was not understood, it has certainly been clarified by the sailors who sing a ribald song as they make ready to set sail, "Take a bouze short leave

---

[10]   Joseph Kerman, 'A Glimmer from the Dark Ages', ibid, p. 224.
[11]   Robert Savage, 'Producing Dido and Aeneas', ibid, p. 268.

of your nymphs on the / shore, / And silence their mourning / With vows of returning, / But never intending to visit them more."

It would seem Aeneas had reconsidered his plan to "pacify" the queen and alternatively intended to abscond without notice; unexpectedly she discovers his men preparing the ships to set sail when she approaches the docks with her courtiers. He attempts to renew his vows by promising to defy the gods, but to no avail as Dido recognises this as a desperate ploy to regain her favour and avoid her wrath. In effect he displays himself as a snivelling coward, revealing a shallow worthless character, thus rendering his heroic tales in the previous Acts nothing more than a superficial display of bravado, i.e. his stories of valour in Act I which attracted Dido, and the grand display of his hunting trophy, the "Bleeding monster's head," in Act II. Ironically, he fails to defy the "feeble stroke of destiny" as he described. Dido, forced to accept the true nature of his weak character and the unfortunate situation he has created, dismisses him in disgust. The delusion of the romantic grand adventurer has faded, uncovering the 'grand deceiver' the epilogue describes.

This moral tale does not revolve solely around Dido and Aeneas; other characters within the opera exemplified vices as a method to warn the girls of the Chelsea school and to instruct them to be wary. The most obvious are the witches created by Tate who were not characters in the original story of the *Aeneid.* Price points out they may be the catalysts of the tragedy, however, their evil hatred of the queen and their desire to destroy her is unexplained which raises the question of why Purcell and Tate introduced them.[12] Tate uses them to send the false messenger to Aeneas, but the real

---

[12]   Price, 'Dido and Aeneas in Context', ibid, p. 9.

Mercury could have accomplished the task without the intervention of the witches. Furthermore, they overlooked the opportunity for a comic scene, as the messenger appears to be authentic; the witches do not amuse themselves at Aeneas' expense with their impostor. I theorise the witches were created as allegories to depict the vices of hatred, jealousy, and contempt for authority; true evil needs no reason to exist, it simply is and feeds upon itself. The enchantresses state they live solely for the pleasure of committing evil and are used as examples of those who create wanton destruction, "Harm's our delight and mischief all our skill … The Queen of Carthage, who we hate, / As we do all in prosperous state." It is possible the witches' intervention with Dido's demise through their diabolic acts was used to exemplify how horrible these particular vices are, and thus discourage the girls from engaging in, or entertaining notions of jealousy and hatred. Intriguingly, they did not portray the witches as 'monstrous beings' as we generally perceive their kind; in contrast, they are presented as normal everyday people who can mingle in society unrecognised without drawing attention to their occult status. They dance with the sailors and have no need to conceal themselves. Is this a reminder for the young ladies to be aware of the company they keep?

Other characters may also represent danger, namely Belinda and the members of Dido's court. They represent enticements of worldly materialism and the shallow sycophantic nature of courtly life. Belinda and Dido's courtiers are eager to assume what the Fates have destined, "The greatest blessing Fate can give, / Our Carthage to secure, and Troy revive," and they are enthusiastic with the prospect of their future wealth, prosperity and importance as Belinda states,

"Empire growing, / Pleasures flowing / Fortune smiles and so should you." Apparently, they are attempting to persuade Dido into making a commitment purely for material gain and their personal welfare. Dido, coerced by their grand aspirations, believes their union could be the fulfilment of Aeneas' quest in establishing a flourishing new empire. Belinda is a perfect example of a false friend; disregarding the knowledge that Dido has reservations and apprehensions concerning his quest, Belinda takes it upon herself to encourage Aeneas to pursue the queen. Ironically, she is the one whom Dido turns to for comfort on her funeral pyre, not realising that Belinda may have precipitated this woeful tragedy. As a sardonic touch, the chorus which acclaimed the prosperous union of Dido and Aeneas with cries of "Cupid strew your path with flowers," now beckons the cupids to scatter roses over her tomb for the finale.

The final major alteration to the original plot concerns the nature of Dido's death. They modified her death to accommodate a school performance — suicide would have been a scandalous immoral act punishable by immediate damnation according to Christian theology, and to portray Dido's death in this manner would have been unconscionable and simply out of the question. In the plot, there is no suggestion that her death was particularly violent or graphic as in Virgil's *Aeneid*, Tate reconstructed the plot in such a manner as to allow the assumption her death resulted from a broken heart. The Sorceress' words "Elisa bleeds tonight," may simply be poetic license and not imply the physical nature of Dido's death.

In review, we observe tempters, sycophants, and menacing situations literally surround Dido; all of which depicts the perilous occasions and immoral vices the young ladies of the school would need to recognise and avoid. Convincingly, this opera was an edifying work intended to instruct, warn, advise and promote high moral and ethical standards that the school wished to maintain. The question arises, why would they choose Virgil's *Aeneid* for this particular entertainment as it obviously contained very graphic and sensitive material requiring a dramatic re-write for this occasion? Dryden's dedication attached to his translation of the *Aeneid* offers a possible clue to this enigma. He states:

> "But he [Aeneas] is arraign'd with more shew of reason by the ladies, who will make a numerous party against him, for being false to love, in forsaking Dido. And I cannot much blame them; for, to say the truth, 'tis an ill precedent for their gallants to follow. Yet, if I can bring him [Aeneas] off with flying colors, they may learn experience at her cost, and, for her sake, avoid a cave, as the worst shelter they can choose from a shower of rain, especially when they have a lover in their company."[13]

It may be possible Virgil's classic was deemed by contemporary women as a symbol of love betrayed. By electing this subject for a moral entertainment, they cunningly chose an appealing topic where the young ladies would readily commiserate with the plight of the queen, and therefore may be less inclined to disregard the message intended to edify. This would also support the

---

[13]   John Dryden, translator, *Virgil's Aeneid*, Charles W. Eliot, ed., *The Harvard Classics*, Vol. 13, (New York: P.F. Collier and Son Corp., 1963), p. 29.

theory they portrayed Dido as a maiden to encourage the girls to further identify with her character as mentioned previously.

To this point, I have endeavoured to demonstrate *Dido and Aeneas* was never intended to be performed for the general public and was specifically written for a private school function; there may have been no further plans to produce it publicly.

It may have been an unfortunate coincidence they considered the subject matter politically sensitive due to the allegorical reference of the monarchs William and Mary. The king and queen celebrated their coronation on April 11, 1689 as we have noted earlier. In accordance with obligatory tradition, Tate praised the two monarchs in the prologue; Phoebus the sun god represents William, while Venus symbolises Mary. Tate may not have intended this allegory to continue into the drama proper; the prologue apparently does not develop or contribute further material to the plot. I suspect it may have been another unfortunate coincident that the lines "when monarchs unite, how happy their fate" sung by the worldly courtiers as a symbol of a union for material gain would appear as an obvious allegory of William and Mary's reign. Purcell and Tate must have realised when they arranged this work for the school they could never have produced it as a public entertainment. We perceive this realisation may account for the deliberate suppression of the score.

In conclusion, theorising the intended purposes of the opera, presented as a morally edifying entertainment solely for the benefit of the Chelsea students and attending families, we are not surprised they dramatically changed the graphic nature of the original story from the *Aeneid* for this one-time occasion, and did not consider further productions at that time. Purcell died in November of 1695, and *Dido and Aeneas* apparently disappeared for five years after his death. We can assume the Theatre Royal in Drury Lane, which was in possession of his works, apparently did not acquire a copy of this opera for their rivals at Lincoln's-Inn staged the first revival.[14] The reaction of Purcell's contemporaries to his opera is exhibited by the fact *Dido and Aeneas* was first revived in combination with Shakespeare's play *Measure for Measure* in 1700. Price maintains this reconstruction as recorded in Gildon's playbook indicates a deliberate attempt to exploit the illicit elements of the *Aeneid*, which Tate had obscured.[15] This supports the theory the public may not have accepted Purcell and Tate's alterations to Virgil's original classic. If Purcell had lived longer and had wished to stage the opera for the public, it would have been necessary to reconstruct the opera for audience approval. Upon reviewing the history of *Dido and Aeneas*, the assumed suppression of the opera is no longer a mysterious occurrence, and the adaptation masquerading as an original revival, is comprehensible.

☙ ✦ ❧

---

[14] Price, 'Dido and Aeneas in Context', *Norton Score, pp. 12-13*.
[15] Ibid. p. 14.

Hogarth, Handel, and 'The Levée' from 'The Rake's Progress': A Satirical Portrait Worth a Thousand Words

William Hogarth's *The Rake's Progress* (completed 1734) is a fascinating series of eight paintings depicting the artist's cynical view of London society. In sequence, the pictures portray the fictitious story of Tom Rakewell, a young man who has inherited a substantial fortune from his miserly father. Having little or no experience in handling money, Tom embarks on a life of debauchery. These pictures relate his 'progression' from a life of wanton vice to abject poverty, ultimately ending his days in the notorious insane asylum, Bedlam.

The second painting of the series entitled *The Rake's Levée* may be of particular interest to Handel scholars. The Rake, now a man of society, is busy squandering his newly gained wealth to acquire a genteel façade in keeping with his new worldly status. However, the tradesmen who attend to his requirements are only interested in relieving Tom of the burden of his newfound wealth. The figure seated at the harpsichord is identified as Handel; the initials F. H. are painted on the score he apparently is presenting to Tom. The figures surrounding Tom may depict several recognisable contemporaries. The man brandishing the *fluret* sword may be the fencing master Dubois; next to him stands a man holding what appears to be quarter-staffs and thereby has been recognised as the prize fighter James Figg.[16] The gentleman in the background holding the large leather-bound book on Tom's right is thought to be Charles Bridgeman, a member of Lord Burlington's social circle; perhaps he is suggesting to the Rake he acquire a country estate.[17]

The remaining sycophants include a man recognised as a French dance master due to his extravagant attire and pose (middle foreground), a huntsman blowing his horn, a kneeling jockey presenting a trophy he won at Epsom for riding his mount 'Silly Tom' to victory, and a hired assassin presenting a letter of introduction reading "Sr. the Capt. is a Man of Honour. his Sword may Serve you Yrs. Wm. Stab." Tom's interest in this dubious figure portrays his lack of wisdom and worldly intelligence, and presents an ill omen for his future. In the background, an additional group of tradesmen wait patiently to be received by the Rake.

Tom's pretence of gentility and his misconceived aristocratic aspirations is evident by his uncouth preference in art. A mediocre painting of foreign manufacture entitled *The Judgement of Paris* has been sold to Tom as a masterpiece, which he has distastefully displayed between portraits of his gamecocks.[18]

This is the traditionally accepted interpretation of *The Rake's Levée*; however, on closer inspection, we may detect a greater significance in its historical symbolism. This painting was completed in 1733–34, the opera season which witnessed Handel's relocation to Covent Garden and the formation of the Opera of the

---

[16] Neil McWilliam, *Hogarth* (London: Studio Editions, 1993), p. 66.
[17] Ibid.
[18] Sean Shesgreen, ed., *Engravings by Hogarth; 101 Prints* (New York: Dover Publications Inc., 1973), # 29.

Engraving of the 'The Levée'

Nobility company; possibly, Hogarth sarcastically depicted this contemporary operatic upheaval in London.

In 1729, after the Royal Academy of Music folded, John Jacob Heidegger, the manager of the King's Theatre in the Haymarket, entered into an agreement with Handel whereby they would continue the production of Italian opera in London for at least five years. The company splintered in 1733 as tensions mounted between Handel and the castrato Senesino; accordingly, Handel dismissed the troublesome performer, who immediately joined the rival company formed by previous directors of the Royal Academy, including Lord Burlington and several members of his circle. Later, Heidegger leased the King's Theatre to the rival company, forcing Handel to seek a different venue after July 1734, namely, Covent Garden managed by John Rich. Consequently, fierce competition emerged between the Nobility Opera and Handel's company at Covent Garden. Unfortunately for Handel, the rival company was openly supported by the Prince of Wales and thereby was considered fashionable by the public. The rival directors had also achieved considerable theatrical *coups* by enticing other singers away from Handel's company, and instrumentalists from his orchestra including the trumpeter Valentine Snow.[19] The rival company had also managed to engage the famous castrato Farinelli for their second season commencing in December of 1734. Handel had employed two castrati, Scalzi and Carestini, in an attempt to compete with the new company, yet Farinelli eclipsed all their endeavours.

---

[19] Christopher Hogwood, *Handel* (New York: Thames and Hudson Inc.,1984, 1988, 1995), p. 125.

Hogarth may have depicted the rivalry of the two companies in *The Rake's Levée*, apparently, both factions are attempting to persuade Tom Rakewell to sponsor their opera company. The two gamecocks may actually represent Paolo Rolli's satirical verses concerning Handel's employment of Scalzi and Carestini and his dismissal of Senesino:

Rolli's Satirical Verses on Carestini, (?) 1734

Che Scalzi e Carestin, que due Campioni
vengan per Handel, non è già una favola :
chè quell grand' Uom mai non si pone a tavola
senza un piatto di due grossi Capponi.

Ma il mandar via questo Cappone è un fallo,
fallo cagionator di sue ruine,
perchè il mio Senesin estimato è un Gallo
di tutte le Brittaniche Galline.

[Those two champions, Scalzi and Carestini, have come to Handel because that great man does not sit down to table without a dish of two fat capons. But to send away this capon would be a mistake that would undo him, for my Senesino is reckoned the cock of all British chickens.][20]

---

[20] Otto Erich Deutsch, *Handel: a Documentary Biography* (New York, Da Capo Press, 1974), p. 341. Sources, (Cellesi, 1930, p. 320.) Manuscript in Biblioteca Comunale, Siena.

Rolli, the Italian librettist who supported Senesino, subsequently joined the Opera of the Nobility. The fact Hogarth placed a picture depicting *The Judgement of Paris* between the gamecocks reinforces the idea that our young Rake must decide between the opera companies. According to Greek mythology, Eris, the goddess of discord, rivalry and competition, attends the marriage of Peleus and Thetis. Eris creates a disturbance by tossing 'the Apple of Discord' between the goddesses and claims only the most beautiful may pick it up. Hera, Athena, and Aphrodite are brought before Paris who will decide which of the three may hold the apple. However, Aphrodite bribes Paris with the promise that Helen of Troy would be his, thus the legendary Trojan War commences. In essence, it is a myth concerning the process of making wise and informed decisions.

We note that Handel was obviously at Covent Garden at this time; observe the title of the opera he is playing, "The Rape of the Sabines." Handel did not compose an opera by this title; however, it is reminiscent of a pantomime entitled *The Rape of Proserpine* (1726) for which John Rich wrote a special dedication. He proposed that Italian opera should be reformed to suit English tastes and therefore "establish that entertainment on a lasting Foundation."[21] In this dedication, he also stated that to assist this adaptation of opera for England, the other arts should also be included. Sarah McCleave states this dedication remained virtually unchanged during the various revivals of this pantomime in the 1730s and apparently, this

---

[21] John Rich, dedication, *The Rape of Proserpine; as it is Acted at the Theatre Royal in Lincoln's Inn-Fields. Written by Theobald, and set to Musick by Mr. Galliard*, 5th ed. (London: T. Wood, 1731: iii-vi. In Sarah McCleave, *Dance in Handel's Operas: The Collaboration with Marie Sallé*, PhD (University of London, King's College, 1993.) pp. 60–62.

was a familiar article to his contemporaries. Handel attempted to integrate the various arts, namely Italian opera with French ballet, at Covent Garden with his *Terpsicore*, *Ariodante*, and *Alcina* featuring the dancer Marie Sallé. Hogarth may have referred to Handel's new French / Italian style with the bogus title "Rape of the Sabines" and hoped his contemporaries would recognise the similarity with the pantomime *The Rape of Proserpine* and Rich's dedication. This association may be reinforced by a new interpretation of the character beside Handel presumed to be a French dance master; notice that he is holding a violin. This figure bears a surprising resemblance to the violinist in Hogarth's engraving *The Enraged Musician* (1741); according to Burney, this was none other than Handel's leading violinist, Pietro Castrucci.[22] Apparently, Hogarth has painted Handel's violinist, and also depicts him in a dance pose, thus displaying the cosmopolitan Italian / French style Handel had adopted.

As we re-examine the characters on Tom's right, the trumpeter may also be re-interpreted; this figure may symbolise the instrumentalist Valentine Snow who deserted Handel in favour of the Nobility Opera. Of notable interest, the foreground scene upon this examination resembles the layout of the artwork behind; the two factions supporting the opera houses flank Tom on his right and left similar to the two fighting cockerels placed on either side of the picture featuring Paris, who apparently has made his choice. (Aphrodite approaches with Cupid and the other goddesses are placed offside, one has her back turned to us.) The fact Handel is placed

---

[22] Hogwood, *Handel*, illustration number 31, p.115.

Engraving of 'The Enraged Musician'

far away from the crowd and also has his back turned to us, we assume the Rake has chosen the rival company supported by Lord Burlington whom Hogarth detested, explaining the Rake's ill-fated attention with the assassin who is conveniently located on the 'rival side' of the painting. Thus, the tasteless art display in the background which Tom Rakewell has been deceived into admiring as a masterpiece mirrors his 'uncouth' choice of opera company, and therefore music, as he is duped into believing it was the 'fashionable' one to attend.

If this was not immediately apparent, Hogarth clarified his intentions with his engraving of the same painting completed a year later, June 1735. He added two additional details; a long written list is draped behind Handel's chair, and a book with a picture of Farinelli emblazoned on the cover sits on the floor. The list reads; "A List of rich Presents Signor Farinelli the Italian Singer Condescended to Accept of ye English Nobility and Gentry for one Nights Performance in the Opera Artaxerses — A pair of Diamond Knee Buckles Presented by — A Diamond Ring by — A Bank Note enclosed in a Rich Gold Case by — A Gold Snuff box Chace'd with the Story of Orpheus Charming ye Brutes by T. Rakewell Esq. 100[£] 20[0£] 100[£]."[23] The opera *Artaxerses* opened the second season of the Nobility Opera company; apparently, our young Rake attended this opening night for he too has donated a costly present. The book features a title page inscribed "A Poem dedicated to T. Rakewell Esq," and included with the picture of Farinelli are a group of women paying 'homage' to their idol by crying the famous exclamation "One G-d, one Farinelli" as two hearts burn below the performer.[24] A lady

---

[23] Shesgreen, *Engravings*, #29.
[24] Ibid.

who attended the opening performance of *Artaxerses,* overcome by Farinelli's voice, first proclaimed this declaration.

Apparently, Hogarth painted an in-depth, cryptic observation of London opera culture and included his own opinions concerning the opera companies on canvas which is difficult to determine unless familiar with the contemporary social and cultural circles. The dissolution of the Royal Academy and the formation of the different companies created quite a stir both socially and politically and was a major topic in what would be considered 'the news headlines' today. Contemporary audiences would have recognised this pictorial satire, which apparently was obscured to us until now. Truly, *The Rake's Levée* proved to be a picture worth a thousand words, or more.

∾✦∽

The Symphonies of Beethoven:
Historical and Philosophical Reflections through
Music

We accept that Beethoven's symphonies are a product of his times and generally reflect the cultural, social, and political environment from which they emerged. Despite this acknowledgement it is evident Beethoven's works are not infallibly indicative of historical occurrences and sequential events; they were ultimately a medium of personal expression and as such may be considered his personal commentary or philosophical chronicles expressed through music. Consequently, when examining these works, a completely accurate portrait of history is not presented; alternatively, we are contemplating contemporary events presented as fragmented glimpses of historical facts mingled with personal interpretations and philosophical perceptions by the composer. By examining a selection of his symphonies in chronological order we may deduce how his perception relating to contemporary events and social changes evolved through his music.

    › Symphony No. 1 in C major, Op. 21
(1800; Dedicated to Baron van Swieten)

    › Symphony No. 2 in D Major, Op. 36
(1801–1802; Dedicated to Prince Lichnowsky)

When we consider the dedications of these symphonies, we are introduced to the aristocratic circle Beethoven socialised in and those who may have influenced him. Baron van Swieten receives Beethoven's first symphonic dedication; one of the important promoters of the 'serious music' culture of Vienna and the philosophical concept of the 'genius-composer'.[25] Prince Lichnowsky, the recipient of the dedication of Symphony No. 2, was also one of the promoters of this music culture.[26] As a diplomat to Berlin in 1769, Baron van Swieten was influenced by the *Sturm und Drang* movement already well established promoting the notion of glorifying the emotions in opposition to the ideals of the Age of Enlightenment that endorsed scientific methods and the primacy of reason.[27] The concepts of the 'creative-genius' and 'organic growth' with regard to creative works first developed in Northern Germany during the 1770s and 1780s.[28] These ideals were fuelled by the translation of a first-century Greek treatise attributed to Longinus entitled *On the Sublime*.[29] This treatise outlines Longinus' views on genius, inspiration, and the characteristics denoting those of 'noble minds'. According to Longinus, the 'Sublime' stems from five sources; the ability to form grand conceptions, the stimulus of powerful and inspired emotion, an appropriate use of figurative language, noble diction and imagery, and the arrangement of words

---

[25] Dr. Christopher Morris, Classical Period Lectures *'The Symphonies of Beethoven'*, October 27 1998.
[26] Ibid.
[27] Tia De Nora, 'Beethoven and the Construction of Genius', *Musical Politics in Vienna,1729–1803*, (Berkeley, University of California Press, 1995), p. 23.
[28] Ibid. p. 23.
[29] Lectures, October 13, 1998.

in speech leading to a total effect of dignity and elevation.[30] Whereas these ideals centred within the literary circles, the musical life of Berlin in the 1700s also reflected these theories of artistic greatness.[31] The *Sturm und Drang* period was influenced by Edmund Burke's work *A Philosophical Enquiry into the origin of our ideas of the Sublime and the Beautiful.* (London 1757) which expanded the theory of the 'Sublime' by comparing it with the wonders of nature. He characterises the 'Sublime' as large and unfathomable, rough and rugged, terrifying and painful, without actually experiencing this intangible state; for instance, we can be terrified by an earthquake without having to live through the actual experience. In effect, the 'sublime' cannot be comprehended but marvelled at, while 'Beauty' is comprehensible and pleasurable, remaining 'small' and 'smoothly-polished'.[32] Immanuel Kant in his work *Critique of Judgement* (Berlin / Libau 1790) supported Burke's philosophy, but preferred to categorise the infinite and unfathomable as the 'mathematically sublime', and the 'terrifying' element as the 'dynamically sublime'.[33] In addition, we observe the expressive free-form *Phantasie* circulating at this time in Northern Germany.[34]

We know Baron van Swieten joined the local music circle in Berlin for he encouraged the promotion of C. P. E. Bach's music and subsequently introduced it to music publishers in Vienna.[35] When van Swieten returned to Vienna in 1777, the ideals associated with the *Sturm und Drang* movement were in the process of development,

---

[30] Ibid.
[31] *Construction of Genius*, p. 24.
[32] Lectures, 1998.
[33] Ibid.
[34] *Construction of Genius*, ibid.
[35] Ibid.

and he promoted these new concepts with a small group of supporters. The first indications of this 'noble style', as Tia De Nora points out, appear in the later works of Mozart c.1780s. Mozart collaborated with van Swieten at this time, and a noticeable change in his music emerged. His later compositions reflected difficult styles, as in counterpoint, and received mixed reviews by audiences.[36] During the Gallant and early Classical period, the heavily ornamented Baroque fugal method was frequently circumvented in favour of a lyrical style — the former was considered an antiquated style associated with church music, and therefore assumed the status of high art. One writer for the *Magazin der Musik*, a long time admirer who formerly praised Mozart's work, wrote in 1787:

> "The most skilful and best keyboard scholar I
> have ever heard; the pity is only that he aims too high
> in his artful and truly beautiful compositions, in order
> to become a new creator, whereby it must be said that
> feeling and heart profit little."[37]

De Nora asserts this indicates the momentum van Swieten and his minority group were achieving in the cultural circles of Vienna.

Ironically, the ideals of the 'Sublime' promoted by van Swieten and his associates blossomed and flourished in the most unexpected manner. This transpired with the dissolution of the aristocratic Hofkapelle and Hauskapellen where the nobility patronised private orchestras for their own entertainment, not

---

[36] Ibid. pp. 13–15.
[37] Ibid. p. 13.

41

caused by an impoverished aristocracy, but attributed to the fashionable changes in Austria.[38] The Imperial Court no longer considered their Hofkapelle exclusive due to the numerous Hauskapellen patronised by the nobility imitating the Imperial Court, and as a result, the Hofkapelle disbanded. The nobility considered this a fashionable statement and followed the Imperial example by dissolving their Hauskapellen.[39]

When Beethoven arrived in Vienna in 1792, the once fashionable Hauskapellen had disappeared completely.[40] Musicians were patronised by the wealthy middle classes of Vienna and this posed a threat for the nobility; they believed they were losing their musical privileges for their once exclusive territory was now 'invaded'. Many amateurs became involved with public performances and the nobles considered the standard of music may deteriorate to cater for their 'class' and the tastes of the 'common man'.

These developments worried van Swieten who declared, "I see a loss in the Sublime of music," and he endeavoured to counteract this wave of events.[41] He patronised composers he considered 'noble' musicians to ensure 'noble music' would continue to propagate, and regarded Beethoven a perfect solution.[42] The nobility controlled many of the important functions of the public theatres to ensure the

---

[38] Lectures, October 27, 1998.
Construction of Genius, p. 40.
[39] Lectures, ibid.
Construction of Genius, p. 41.
[40] Ibid. p. 40.
[41] Lectures, October 17, 1998.
[42] Ibid.

middle classes would not have distinctive power or influence in the area of patronage.[43]

Why did van Swieten and the nobility choose Beethoven? Convincingly, it was not luck, nor the opportune timing of his arrival in Vienna, but rather his ideology and character that influenced this choice. Beethoven was familiar with the writing and ideals held by Kant on the 'Sublime' and the 'Beautiful' and he was influenced by this philosophy. Beethoven once quoted Kant, " ... two things fill the mind with ever new and increasing admiration and awe, the more often and steadily we contemplate them; the starry heavens above me, and the moral law within me."[44] Beethoven was 'stormy' and 'rugged' in character with Burke's description of all things 'Sublime'; Beethoven was described as rude and blunt, considering himself of noble origin, never stepping aside for aristocrats as they passed him in the streets for he considered himself their equal. Baron Peter von Braun, manager of the Theatre an der Wien in 1806, asked Beethoven to compose in a manner which would appeal to the general public and thus fill the house and increase ticket sales — Beethoven retorted, "I don't write for the galleries!"[45] He considered himself a member of the nobility for during the custody dispute concerning his nephew Karl he decided to have the trial held at the court reserved for the aristocracy, claiming that his name 'von Beethoven' signified noble birth and entitled him to this privilege. I theorise Beethoven deemed an association with the aristocracy signified an affinity with all things 'Sublime' — perhaps he concluded that to socialise with the nobles and interact with those

---

[43] Ibid. October 13, 1998.
[44] Ibid.
[45] *Construction of Genius*, p. 8.

43

considered of 'noble intellect' he would also be numbered with the elite. This may explain his endeavour to remain autonomous within the music scene; he elevated his status as a musician generally considered a subservient occupation to the nobility or religious establishments.

Returning to the concept of 'Sublimity' in music, the symphony as a genre was considered the only form where the 'Sublime' could be expressed. J. A. P. Schulz who contributed to Sulzer's *General Theory of the Fine Arts* discussed this ideology in the 1770s. Judging from Beethoven's symphonic production rate, e.g. eight symphonies composed from 1800 to 1812, it is obvious, this genre was in great demand by the nobility who patronised him. Schulz wrote:

> "The symphony is excellently suited for the expression of the grand, the festive, and the sublime [...]. The allegros of the best chamber symphonies contain great and bold ideas, free handling of composition, seeming disorder in the melody and harmony, strongly marked rhythms of different kinds, powerful bass melodies and unisons, concerting middle voices, free imitations, often a theme that is handled in a manner of a fugue, sudden transitions and digressions from one key to another [...] strong shadings of the forte and the piano, and chiefly of the crescendo."[46]

---

[46] Lectures, October 13, 1998.

Evidently, Beethoven considered these ideals, for his symphonic music contains many of these characteristics; let us focus on the exposition of the first movement from Symphony No. 1.

In the slow introduction, we may observe characteristics of this 'Sublime' style before the commencement of the allegro! Short phrases alternate between *forte* and *piano* (Bars 1–2), leading into a short *crescendo* followed by *forte* (Bars 3–4). The strings introduce a melody in *piano* (Bars 5–7), which is proceeded by a short *tutti* passage with *forte* chords dynamically labelled *tenuto* which interrupt the rhythm (Bars 8–11). The allegro proper commences in *piano* (Bar 13), followed by another *crescendo* passage (Bars 23–45). Throughout the exposition, we see examples of his use of *crescendo*, and alternating dynamic passages of *forte* and *piano*, *f* (Bars 45–52), *p* (Bars 53–56), *f* (Bars 57–61), *p* (Bars 62–65). At Bars 53–56, we observe an imitation of melody between the oboes and flutes, proceeded by a syncopated passage featuring overlapping phrases in the string and woodwind sections at Bars 65–67. A section that abruptly modulates from G major at Bars 76–77 into C minor, and immediately returns to G major at Bars 82–88, follows this passage. Here in this minor key, we perceive the 'darker' side of Beethoven's music, an element that may be considered an aspect of the 'terrifying', unexpected nature of the 'Sublime'.

Within his first symphony, we detect elements that were characterised as the 'Sublime' within the symphonic form. Apparently, his patrons recognised these characteristics, accordingly they referred to him as a 'noble' composer. Considering the 'small' size of his first symphony in comparison with his later symphonies, and the fact that it was comprehensible to his audience, may we

45

assume Beethoven was embarking upon a quest for the 'infinite' or the 'mathematically sublime'? As he composed each successive symphony, his style became more complex and his patrons found them difficult to comprehend. On an examination of Symphony No. 2, we notice a definite evolution in his style.

Within the first eight bars, we again observe examples of alternating *forte* and *piano* sections using various degrees of the dynamic scale. We also notice strongly marked rhythms such as double-dotted quaver and dotted semiquaver rhythms followed by semiquaver triplets in Bar 7, which are proceeded by semiquaver and demisemiquaver scalic 'runs' alternating in the woodwinds and strings (Bars 12–16). The next section features scalic 'runs' which are imitated between the first violins and the 'cellos / double basses (Bars 17–22). These scalic passages serve an interesting purpose; they are aurally deceptive due to the change in rhythm — the listener assumes the allegro proper has commenced, while in fact, the slow introduction has not yet concluded. This passage in the symphony is unpredictable and therefore may be considered similar to the unexpected 'terrifying' elements of the 'Sublime' that Burke describes. Other 'Sublime' examples are found in Bars 34–35, where the first subject is introduced in the bass section, thus fulfilling the criteria of 'powerful bass melodies' as described by Schulz. We also notice strongly marked syncopated rhythms in the woodwind section (Bars 41–45), and alternations of *forte* and *piano* dynamics combined with melodic / motivic passages in the bass section (Bars 71–85). In the development section, we observe his use of contrapuntal writing in the strings (Bars 86–96), which corresponds to Schulz's description of themes "handled in a manner of a fugue."

In summary, Beethoven's first two symphonies reflect the social and cultural changes occurring in Vienna such as the emergence of 'Serious' music patronage, and the promotion of the ideology expounding the 'Sublime'.

On an examination of his succeeding three symphonies, our horizons broaden, revealing his personal philosophy expressed through his music combined with his possible outlook concerning the major historical events of the time.

- ૐ Symphony No. 3 E Flat Major Op. 55, "Eroica" (1803; dedicated to Prince Lobkowitz)

- ૐ Symphony No. 5 (1807 – 1808)

- ૐ Symphony No. 6 "Pastoral" (1808)

The title of Symphony No. 3, "Eroica," translated 'hero', enables us to view the historical context combined with the philosophical theories of the 'Sublime'. May we consider a 'hero', a man who distinguishes himself above all others through struggle to ultimately triumph, the human equivalent of the 'Sublime'? Originally, this work was dedicated to Napoleon, however, when Beethoven heard he had crowned himself Emperor of France, he obliterated the dedication on the title page. This action expressed the disillusionment concerning Napoleon throughout Europe. During the time of the French Revolution, the philosophy of the Enlightenment circulated throughout Europe, i.e. where all mankind would be free and equal, and through the process of reason could form a just society. When Napoleon autocratically crowned himself, this ideal was shattered. Beethoven declared, "Is he too nothing more than human? Now he will crush the rights of man. He will become a tyrant!"[47] Upon the publication of the "Eroica" symphony in 1805, Beethoven inserted a new dedication with the inscription, "To celebrate the memory of a great man."

According to Maynard Solomon, Beethoven's reaction is not the first indication of his frustrations with Napoleon.[48] In 1796–97 he set an anti-Napoleonic text by Friedelburg and composed a German patriotic song. In 1801, Beethoven was furious with Napoleon for signing the Concordat with the Vatican; he believed this signalled the return to former ecclesiastical rule, and that progress in social freedoms would therefore be stifled. Considering his growing disapproval, why did Beethoven initially dedicate the "Eroica" to Napoleon? Solomon believes Beethoven's original dedication to Bonaparte indicates his hope of obtaining a position in France; the possibility of war reoccurring in 1805 dashed this hope. Solomon maintains Beethoven's loyalty to Napoleon and Austria wavered depending on the social climate until Napoleon was finally defeated. The first "Eroica" dedication may signal Beethoven's sense of opportunism.

This incident may also be a clue to Beethoven's philosophy regarding Enlightenment ideology in conjunction with that of the 'Sublime'. As previously noted, he preferred to associate with the nobility rather than the 'common man', but he also recognised their failings, as with Napoleon's autocratic behaviour. Peaceful

---

[47] *The Great Composers: Beethoven* (London: Marshall Cavendish Ltd., 1995), p. 7.
[48] Maynard Solomon, *Beethoven* (Schirmer Books, 1979).

brotherhood could not exist as long as a tyrant ruled. Beethoven may have viewed Napoleon's motives emanated from a selfish and despotic nature, characteristics a 'noble mind' should never entertain. Therefore, we can assume this was his philosophy; the 'Sublimity' of a noble mind can be attained by the use of reason and intellect, and thereby all men could be truly liberated and a just society could exist.

This symphony, in contrast to the first and second, is of epic proportion and received varied responses. Perhaps it would have been fitting if Beethoven had called it the 'Ironica Symphony'; it was misunderstood by those who claimed to believe in the principles of the 'Sublime', yet, it contained more elements of the 'Sublime' than his previous two symphonies. If the 'Sublime' was characterised as 'unfathomable' and of 'gigantic proportions' did not Beethoven fulfil this expectation with the length of the "Eroica?" For example, the Coda in the first movement was the longest he had composed at that point. The "Eroica" was difficult to understand for Beethoven also extended the range of 'hearing in time' as Charles Rosen points out:

> "… the extension of the range of hearing in time is remarkable; the dissonant C-sharp in the seventh measure finds its full meaning only much later at the opening recapitulation, when it becomes a D-flat and leads to an F-major horn solo."[49]

---

[49] Charles Rosen, *The Classical Style, Haydn, Mozart, Beethoven* (London: Faber and Faber, 1971), pp. 393–394.

Critics complained of the length of the work and claimed it lacked unity![50] This claimed 'lack of unity' originated from Beethoven's use of 'cell-blocks' to construct his subjects replacing long flowing melodies; this method facilitated the expansion of the symphonic form as a unit of 'organic growth'. Theoretically, could these minute motifs reflect the 'rugged' elements of the 'Sublime', while in contrast, melodic passages could be referred to as the 'polished element' of the 'Beautiful'? Perhaps Beethoven's apparent success in capturing the essence of the 'terrifying' and 'overpowering' nature of the 'Sublime' by this method may be affirmed by the confusion of his audiences. Beethoven's work had become 'unfathomable', i.e. the composer distances himself from the audience; now the listener was compelled to extend his knowledge of the composer to understand the lofty aspirations portrayed in the music. Ultimately, we behold the emergence of the 'artist-composer'. A critic once remarked of Beethoven's music:

> "... it could reach the point where one would derive no pleasure from it unless well trained in the rules and difficulties of the art, but rather, would leave the concert hall ... crushed by a mass of unconnected and overloaded ideas and a continuing tumult of all the instruments."[51]

The idea of the 'artist-composer' allows us to experience the 'Sublime' in music; study was required to obtain an understanding and appreciation of the composer's art. Initially, Beethoven's

---

[50] Ibid. pp. 392–393.
[51] Ibid. p. 393.

symphonies appear like the infinite 'starry heavens' he referred to, and they inspire us with awe. On further reflection, we attempt to appreciate what he was aspiring to express as an artist through music.

This may account for the various interpretations of his work, ranging from the analytical to the poetical. Many critics due to the programmatic title and the unusual funeral movement have interpreted the "Eroica" as a symbol of a hero's inner-struggle. The term 'hero' may also refer to Beethoven; in the early 1800s, he noticed his hearing was beginning to deteriorate. In 1801 Beethoven wrote to his friend Wegeler concerning his initial reactions to this malady, "No! I cannot endure it. I will seize Fate by the throat. It will not wholly conquer me!"[52] When he discovered his hearing would not improve he wrote of his despair in 1802:

> "O you men who accuse me of being malevolent, stubborn and misanthropical, how you wrong me! You know not the secret cause. Ever since childhood, my heart and mind were disposed towards feelings of greatness and good will and I was eager to accomplish great deeds; but consider this; for six years I have been hopelessly ill, aggravated and cheated by quacks in the hope of improving but finally compelled to face a lasting malady ... I was forced to isolate myself. I was misunderstood and rudely repulsed because I was as yet unable to say to people, 'Speak louder, shout, for I am deaf' ... With

---

[52] *Great Composers*, p. 5.

joy I hasten to meet Death. Despite my fate … I wish that it had come later; but I am content, for He shall free me of constant suffering. Come then, Death, and I shall face thee with courage."[53]

Despite his initial depression, Beethoven was still determined to "accomplish great deeds" as a 'Sublime hero', and surpassed his previous works with the monumental "Eroica" Symphony in 1803.

I wish to present an additional viewpoint; the funeral movement may have a twofold significance or dual implication. As mentioned, Beethoven initially intended to praise Napoleon and the ideals of the Enlightenment; the funeral march could symbolise the death of the old European way of life and thereby reflect the birth of a new era. However, Beethoven rededicated the symphony when these hopes faded; the funeral march may be construed as mourning the loss of these ideals and Napoleon as he also mourned "the memory of a great man." The funeral march is constructed in three sections, with the third section interrupted by three smaller sections. [54] The concentration on the number three is fascinating, and it brings to mind the battle cry of the French Revolution; "Liberty, Equality, Fraternity." Was Beethoven endeavouring to create a numerical association with these three sentiments? It would appear there is a parallel with regard to the concept of the philosophical 'hero' and Beethoven as he struggled with his disillusion of the Napoleonic ideal.

Despite Beethoven's disappointment with Napoleon, it would seem he never lost faith in what the French Revolution initially

---

[53]   Ibid. pp. 5–6. Excerpt of the 'Heiligenstadt Testament', 6, October 1802.
[54]   *Lectures*, November 3, 1998.

represented; if we briefly examine the Fifth Symphony, we may observe this faithful persistence. During the French Revolution, music specially composed for outdoor military, festive and ceremonial occasions circulated throughout Europe in various collections as with the *Magasin de musique à l'usage des fêtés nationals* (1794–97). This music, composed for large open-air wind ensembles, is simple and homophonic in style with even 'square' phrasing. Apparently, Beethoven applied this ceremonial style to his compositions that clashed with the classical concept of the 'Sublime.' We notice this particularly at the end of the second movement and in the finale. He used 'square phrasing' thus the music is not 'confined' and our aural perceptions are 'liberated'; we do not hear the overlapping of phrases, nor the overwhelming drive towards cadences that was characteristic of the 'Sublime' style. Apparently, Beethoven had not abandoned his concept of the 'Enlightened Sublime' as we may assume from the revolutionary style he borrowed. Ironically, one may argue this is a contradiction; if Beethoven was not composing according to the perceived qualities of the 'Sublime' with 'overlapping' and 'rugged' phrases as stated earlier, can we characterise this symphony as 'Sublime'? I suggest we may, for his stylistic compositions were becoming unpredictable as experienced with the unforeseen, awesome, 'Sublime' forces of nature.

This unpredictability continues with the "Pastoral" Symphony, which he composed in a completely different style when compared to the Fifth. Beethoven's unpredictability rests with his use of pastoral imagery; the pastoral style was considered antiquated. At that time, the *Sturm und Drang* philosophy whereby music should express actual emotions, and not simply imitate them or the sounds of nature, was the prevailing concept. Interestingly, while Beethoven had returned to an older style, he wished this composition to be viewed in accordance with the current ideals of the time for he wrote, "Even without a description, one will recognise this symphony more as an expression of feeling than a tone painting."[55] Unfortunately, his audiences remained unconvinced and continued to perceive his work 'old-fashioned'.

Which emotions was he endeavouring to express? We do not hear music reminiscent of the Revolution, instead, we are presented with a programmatic work painting a picture of the Elysian Fields; is this Beethoven's yearning for a perfect world with peace, harmony, and brotherhood? In the 'Storm' Movement, we may detect the concept of 'struggle'; surprisingly, Beethoven confined the major turbulence and dissonance within the symphony to this one area. Is Beethoven suggesting that in order to achieve this 'Utopian' dream, we must still undergo that turbulent journey to Hades and back? Although he composed this symphony using elements considered 'out of date', he had created something unique in using the pastoral style. The 'Storm' Movement encapsulates the principal tension of the symphony and acts as a development section of sonata form, with the other movements portrayed as the exposition and the recapitulation. In effect, the symphony achieves the aspect of a one-movement work. Let us for a moment re-examine the concept of the 'Sublime' from a new perspective. Burke described the 'Sublime' by comparing it with the awesome power of natural events; so, let us consider the power of natural forces. It is

---

[55] *Lectures*, November 17, 1998.

acknowledged the face of the earth is constantly changing by the reoccurrences of erosion, fires, droughts, earthquakes, volcanoes, etc., and thereby is in constant state of renewal. Yet, these forces are ancient, they have been in existence from the beginning of time. The same concept may be applied to Beethoven's vision of the 'starry skies' ... they are also ancient, but ever changing. Therefore, one may conclude that all things 'Sublime' in nature are both ancient and new. This phenomenon can also be reflected through music — with the "Pastoral" Symphony, Beethoven had utilised an old style while simultaneously creating something unique.

Apart from the philosophical aspect, are there any indications of historical events depicted within these two symphonies? Perhaps we may recognise events through our own personal interpretations. For instance, the opening motif of the Fifth Symphony and the revolutionary style he incorporated suggests aggression — does this reflect the possibility of war and a time of hardship ahead? In May of 1809, Napoleon captured Vienna; it is logical to assume that the citizens of the town would have been aware of the advancing army. If we consider the optimistic nature of the "Pastoral," could this reflect a renewal of faith in Napoleon as a liberator rather than a future oppressor? Unfortunately, we may never discover Beethoven's true intentions.

❧ Symphony No. 9 in D Minor Op. 125 (1822–24)

Beethoven's last symphony is primarily a treasure-chest of information concerning his personal life and philosophical aspirations. He had surpassed his previous symphonic compositions in structure and originality; for instance, this was the first symphony to include a choral finale and therefore is a major landmark in symphonic writing. The use of text within a genre that was exclusively an instrumental form strongly suggests he composed this symphony with extra-musical associations.

Why did Beethoven choose Schiller's optimistic poem "Ode to Joy" (1785) as the text for the finale? When Beethoven composed the Ninth Symphony, the sentiments expressed in the poem were out of date by thirty years according to contemporary ideology! Apparently, Schiller felt embarrassed by this poem for he did not want it included in the reprinted edition of his works in 1800 stating it was "A bad poem ... written against the bad taste of the age."[56] When the Ninth premiered, Europeans doubted their previous belief in the Enlightenment, especially the Viennese then currently governed by a police state under the rule of Prince Clemens von Metternich.[57] Secret agents roamed the streets, and the general morale of the population suffered as a result; at this time, Beethoven included written answers in his conversation books when out in public for fear of being overheard by the Secret Police.[58] The choice of this joyous text may express 'escapism' and the yearning for happier times.

A twelve-year composition void existed between the Eighth Symphony and the premier of the Ninth; during this time-lapse, Beethoven experienced a series of personal crises. The first

---

[56] Robert Winter, 'The Ninth Symphony', *Microsoft Multimedia Beethoven* (U.S.A.: Microsoft Corporation 1991–1994).
[57] Ibid.
[58] Ibid.

misfortune occurred with a tragic love affair; an emotional letter, dated 1812 and addressed to an anonymous woman referring to her as the "Immortal Beloved," discovered after his death, became public knowledge. Solomon theorises the mysterious "Beloved" was Antonie Brentano, the wife of one of Beethoven's supporters.[59] Beethoven became acquainted with the Brentano family in 1810; during Antonie's frequent illnesses, his music was a source of comfort as he played in an adjacent room. Solomon suggests that a romance had deepened by 1811 when he dedicated his song "An die Geliebte" ("To the Beloved") to her. In the letter of 1812, Beethoven mentions a 'barrier' that separated them; Solomon theorises this indicated Antonie's married state, and in attempting to decipher the meaning, has suggested Antonie may have already expressed her wish to leave her husband and their two children for Beethoven. This decision on her part may have resulted in conflict for Beethoven; many times, he had focused his attentions on women who were of high station and was rejected by them. The idea that Antonie loved him in return and was willing to lose everything to be with him may have proved too difficult to comprehend. Beethoven writes in his letter "Oh continue to love me," Solomon interprets this sentence as his fears of entering into this type of relationship. In accordance with Solomon's ideas, I theorise it is possible Beethoven may have considered this situation incomprehensible due to the manner of the rejections he received. Other women rejected him due to his appearance and rough mannerisms; disfigured in early life by smallpox, they referred to him as 'ugly' and 'coarse', and possibly, he could not understand this

---

[59] Ibid.

unconditional declaration of Antonie's love. At the age of forty-one, Beethoven finally abandoned all plans of marriage.

When Beethoven's brother died in 1815, another stressful situation emerged with the custody battle for his nephew, Karl; Beethoven was convinced his sister-in-law was an unfit parent. As mentioned previously, Beethoven petitioned the court reserved for the aristocrats, however, having to admit he was not of noble lineage, they forced him to refer to the commoners' court. Ultimately, he felt humiliated by this situation and considered he had been publicly disgraced. In addition, the custody case lasted for many years only to yield sour fruit; when Beethoven eventually gained custody of Karl, he proved troublesome believing his uncle was oppressive and overbearing. Karl attempted suicide in 1826; this experience shocked Beethoven.

Finally, Beethoven had to face the challenge of his growing deafness. Initially, his hearing problem was intermittent, but steadily declined as time progressed. By 1817–18 Beethoven was clinically deaf. One can only imagine how difficult it was for him to accept this condition! His woeful experiences combined with his total loss of hearing may account for the twelve-year 'symphonic void'.

Returning to the Ninth Symphony, and having considered these turbulent episodes in his life, Beethoven's use of Schiller's text may appear to us as an act of defiance. He was not willing to surrender to the effects of these tragedies, nor abandon his ideals of the Enlightenment despite the consensus that these concepts were well and truly 'dead'.

Beethoven was composing in an extraordinary manner that perplexed his audiences more than before. Combined with 'old-fashioned' methods, he used modern forms that clashed with the 'Sublime' ideology, introducing extremely original and innovative concepts into the symphonic form. This was the first symphony to incorporate a style associated with opera and to recall themes from previous movements. In the opening ritornello of the fourth movement beginning at Bars 8–16, he uses a bass recitative to introduce and 'reject' restatements of previous themes. In addition, we must not forget Beethoven's inclusion of Schiller's Ode; as mentioned, this was the first time the spoken word was set in a symphony. At Bar 331, Beethoven introduced a Turkish march, a genre that was associated with popular appeal and not with 'serious' music ideology. This is followed by a fugal section at Bar 431, then an archaic chant-like passage at Bar 595, which is further developed into a style reflective of a Mozart mass. The *prestissimo* section of the Coda commencing at Bar 855 concludes the symphony in a style reminiscent of a Rossini opera! Rossini was very popular in Vienna, however due to the 'mass appeal' quality of his music, the 'serious thinkers'dismissed him.

Apparently, we may perceive the 'Sublime artist-composer' at work; audiences failed to comprehend this symphony due to its extraordinary original structure. As discussed previously, the composer and his art required an in-depth study to obtain a true understanding, as with all things considered 'Sublime'. Proof of this compulsive obsession to explain the symphony is abundant as Debussy points out:

"A fog of verbiage and criticism surrounds the
Choral Symphony. It is amazing that it has not been

59

finally buried under the mass of prose which it has provoked. Wagner intended to complete the orchestration. Others fancied that they could explain and illustrate the theme by means of pictures."[60]

May we dare to consider this symphony from an autobiographical viewpoint? Beethoven's teacher in Bonn once said to him, "Unless the composer has in mind a character of a person, his music is nothing more than jingle-jangle."[61] Perchance Beethoven portrayed his own character in this symphony. His use of recitative in the bass of the finale to reintroduce themes from the previous movements may be the key to understanding this work; it is comparable to a meditative 'inner-voice' evoking past memories. These three themes may represent Beethoven's three personal crises. The falling perfect fifth at Bar 30 from the first movement may signify the struggle with his progressive deafness. In the first movement, this falling fifth introduces what Robert Winter describes as the "Defiance Theme."[62] It features dotted quaver passages followed by dotted crotchets written as marked tremolo sextolets proceeded by sextolets. At first, the link between this theme and Beethoven's deafness is not apparent, however, in an early sketch, Beethoven described the first movement of the Ninth Symphony as "Despair."[63] Why did Beethoven christen the movement with this title? If we return to his Second Symphony, we may find a similar theme in Bars 6–33 of the first movement. It features dotted quaver

---

[60] Claude Debussy, 'Monsieur Croche the Dilettante Hater', found in *Three Classics in the Aesthetic of Music* (New York: Dover Publications, 1962), p. 16.
[61] Lectures, November 3, 1998.
[62] Winter, *Microsoft, Beethoven*.
[63] Ibid.

passages proceeded by dotted tremolo sextolet crotchets followed by semiquaver triplets similar to the sextolets of the Defiance Theme. Beethoven composed the Second Symphony in the same timeframe he became aware his hearing was in decline; did he associate these two themes with his despair? In the fourth movement of the Ninth symphony, the recitative abruptly interrupts the falling fifth motif and the "Defiance Theme" is not heard; is Beethoven defying his condition?

The scherzo theme at Bar 48 may possibly reflect the fleeting happiness he found in his life, and the slow movement theme at Bar 63 may portray his affair with the "Immortal Beloved." The 'voice' introduces these past experiences and rejects each in turn. Suddenly, a voice interrupts, "Oh, friends, not these sounds! Let us call up ones that are more joyful!" This text is unique for the words are not from Schiller, but inserted by Beethoven. Is it time to forget all mournful thoughts of the past? It would appear so; at this point, we hear the triumphant 'Joy Theme', an indication of courage and a renewal in his former conviction — the ideals he had once believed in were not dead.

Arguably, his use of the Turkish march also portrays his belief in equality and fraternity; he set the text "where all men shall be brothers" within the march, followed by a style comparable to Western sacred music. In the wake of the Napoleonic Wars, interest in the area of Orientalism increased; we know Beethoven was not prejudiced towards Eastern culture as he formed his spiritual beliefs from Eastern religious texts. Perhaps Beethoven was attempting to inform his listeners that all men are created equal; the West considered the East primitive and inferior, yet, Beethoven had identified a 'lowly' Turkish march in the same category as Western sacred music. If this was Beethoven's intention, it was lost on his audiences; some critics were indignant, one had the audacity to remark the opening bassoon passage of the march sounded like flatulent emissions! In addition, it is common knowledge Beethoven did not appreciate Rossini's music, yet, he included a section reflecting his style. Is this a similar reference to lay aside our differences, as we are all brothers?

The next striking passage to consider is Beethoven's setting of "there must be a God." It may be argued that the repetition of the word 'must' indicated Beethoven doubted the existence of God, however, this may be dismissed for he entitled the slow movement of his quartet Op. 132 "A holy song of thanks from a convalescent to God in the Lydian mode." How can you thank God if you do not believe He exists? The repetition of the word 'must' may have several interpretations. Beethoven was 'blunt' in character; this could be a sarcastic reference to his sufferings portrayed in the re-occurring themes — there had better be a Heaven! Yet, if he intended to express a reverent sentiment, this could imply we may achieve true peace through belief in God and the hope of a better hereafter. This latter interpretation appears to be his intention when we examine Bar 639 onward; the chorus and the orchestration soar into the high registers, and the bass becomes non-existent. The chorus proclaims, "Seek Him beyond the canopy of the stars! Beyond the canopy of stars He must live!" At Bar 647, our senses musically transcend Earth's gravity and hover in the weightless atmosphere of space, raised to the height of musical infinity.

One may consider this symphony similar to a star-studded sky and in much the same manner as we view the 'Sublime' wonders of the Earth.   Similar to the monolithic forces of nature that are ancient yet constantly renewed, this symphony with its monumental musical structure, holds the same fascinating and awe-inspiring power, and will remain a treasured classic in Western art-music history.

We may conclude that Beethoven's symphonies were a product of their times and reflected the world as he perceived it. Interpretations by audiences, musicologists, debaters, and music amateurs will prolong the arguments and theories will be ever changing. We may never discern the true and accurate historical picture encrypted within his music, but with hindsight and knowledge of the era, we may continue the attempt to piece together his philosophy and attitude towards the social and cultural environment of his time.

ॐ ✦ ॐ

Liszt, Goethe, the *Faust Symphony*, and the Symphonic Poem: 'The Word Must Become the Deed'

Goethe's literary classic, *Faust*, has seldom failed to mesmerise those who read it; many are held captive by the fundamental intrinsic nature of this work portraying a man's insatiable search for knowledge and happiness, regardless of the cost, even to the ultimate sacrifice of his own immortal soul. This magnetic fascination is possibly explained by the observation this classic tale touches a 'raw nerve', as we perceive a reflection of our own weaknesses and failures polemically combined with our aspirations or higher nature associated with the protagonists of the plot. Goethe's intriguing opus had a spellbinding effect on many composers of the Romantic Era, including Beethoven, Berlioz, Wagner, and Gounod; — Franz Liszt proved no exception as he too fell under the hypnotic power of this compelling story.

The Faust Legend

The tale of Faust has a basis in fact, however, like many legends, the details became clouded through years of storytelling and continual adaptation. The historical Faust, Georgius 'Sabellicus' Faustus (1480? – 1538?), according to the various legends, was a German fortune teller and magician who performed marvels as he travelled though Thuringia.[64]   In 1509, he supposedly received a degree at Heidelberg University, and he was thereafter, referred to as 'Dr. Faustus'.[65]   Rumours related he was a schoolteacher in the various University cities of Germany and many contemporary scholars referred to him as a charlatan.[66]   Several accounts maintain Faustus was patronised by the Archbishop of Cologne in 1532 and accordingly became a citizen of respectability, although this has not been proven. Incidentally, leaders of the Reformation such as Martin Luther believed he had supernatural powers.[67]   By the late sixteenth century, these legends were widely circulated; many tales dating from medieval times relating the powers of pseudoscientists and magicians became synonymous with the name 'Faustus' or 'Faust'.[68]

The first literature entitled *Histora von Dr. Johann Fausten* relating the Faustian legend was printed in Frankfurt in 1587, and featured the original account of Faust's pact with the devil. According to this narrative, the scholar Faust made a compact with the devil; Faust agreed to sell his soul and in return, he would receive the restoration of youth, an increased knowledge of the occult, be granted considerable power and experience all worldly pleasures. This account relates when the allotted time of twenty-four years expired, he repented having sold his soul for illusory knowledge, but

---

[64]   Alan Walker, *Franz Liszt; The Weimar Years, 1848–1861*, Vol. II (New York: Alfred A. Knopf Inc., 1989), p. 328. For more detailed information on the historical Faust, see E.A. Bucchianeri, *Faust: My Soul be Damned for the World   Vol. 1* (Batalha Publishers: 2010).
[65]   Ibid.
[66]   'Faust', *Microsoft Multimedia Encyclopedia Encarta* (U.S.A.: Microsoft Corporation, 1992–1994)
[67]   Ibid.
[68]   Ibid.

to no avail; the devil would not relinquish the compact and dragged his soul to the fiery depths of Hell.

The first translation appeared in English in 1587 and in German verse in 1588, and later in 1592 as written prose with the text in English and French. Christopher Marlowe wrote his famous drama *The Tragedy of Doctor Faustus* in 1589 based on a recent translation of the Faustus legend.[69] English players brought Marlowe's drama to Germany where it was adapted by other drama companies, parodied in farcical productions, and ultimately degenerated to a puppet show. This puppet show introduced Johann Wolfgang von Goethe (1749–1832) to the story, which captured his imagination.[70] For many years, Goethe struggled writing his own adaptation of the legend; the First Part was completed in 1808, and the Second Part was published a year after his death in 1833.

Goethe's version remains the predominant literary account of the Faustian Legend; he introduces the character of Gretchen and the important detail that Faust is not condemned to eternal damnation, but is saved by Gretchen's intercession. We may attribute the appeal of this version to Goethe's apparent personal affiliation with the legendary story and his empathy with Faust's character. Goethe once wrote:

> "The significant puppet-play legend … echoed
> and buzzed in many tones within me. I too had
> drifted about in all knowledge, and early experiments
> in life, and had always come back more unsatisfied

---

[69] Ibid.

[70] Charles W. Eliot, ed., The Harvard Classics, Vol. 19, Johann Wolfgang von Goethe, "Faust, Part I," (New York: P.F. Collier and Son Corporation, 1963), p.6.

and more tormented. I was now carrying these things, like many others, about with me and delighting myself with them in lonely hours, but without writing anything down."[71]

Goethe was haunted by his personal conflicts, and arguably, his apparent struggle to portray them with the character of Faust may have been the key factor in the creation of the "Faustian Conflict." Goethe breathed life into the character of Faust through his own experiences, and thus created a convincing, realistic individual. In Goethe's version of the legend, Faust agrees to sell his soul on one condition; that the devil can prove he has the capability of giving him the happiness and knowledge he seeks. Faust is not predestined for Hell for he uses his soul as the bargaining power enabling him to retain an escape clause. Faust is not portrayed as a demonic character but a man searching to fulfil his ambition to acquire absolute truth through knowledge not attainable to mortal man who is fettered on earth. In the event the devil can comply with the condition of the contract, he must relinquish his soul. Ultimately, Faust represents Man striving to find the true meaning and happiness of life.

Goethe's introduction of Gretchen was inspired by a real-life incident concerning a young woman who had been seduced and abandoned, ultimately killing her illegitimate child. She was condemned to death and her contrite lover joined her in prison to die with her.[72] In Goethe's drama, Faust seduces Gretchen, absolutely

---

[71] Ibid.

[72] Paul Brians, Department of English, Washington State University, September 2000. Website; — http://www.wsu.edu:8080/~brians/hum_303/faust.html

destroying her. She bears his illegitimate child whom she drowns in a tirade of madness, is condemned to death, and Faust attempts to rescue her. In moments of sanity, she realises Faust is in league with the Powers of Darkness, she begs God for forgiveness, and is saved at the conclusion of Part I.

Faust continues his search for knowledge and truth in Part II, and in the process, builds a kingdom on land reclaimed from the sea.[73] When his death approaches, he describes his dream of a land and a people that are free.[74] Faust senses this dream may come true in the future and cries out the fateful sentence, "Stay, thou are fair!" Yet, his soul is not lost for he discovers the true idealistic 'fair' does not yet exist. As a spirit of negation and destruction, the devil is not capable of creating this 'Utopian' dream and cannot grant Faust's desires. The contract cannot be fulfilled and Faust is saved from damnation. The angels state, "Who ever strives with all his power, / we are allowed to save."[75] Gretchen intercedes for his soul, and he is elevated to Heaven by the angels; the last lines of the play read "Eternal womanhood draws us onward."[76] Faust is saved by his ceaseless search for knowledge and truth, and his love for Gretchen.[77]

Goethe's unique interjection of human aspirations and conflicting emotions to the Faustian legend resulted in a drama that we can identify with. We also confront similar temptations and

---

[73] Nicholas Vazonyi, 'Liszt, Goethe, and the Faust Symphony', *Journal of the American Liszt Society,* 40 (1996), p. 2.
[74] Ibid.
[75] Paul Brians, ibid.
[76] Ibid.
[77] For a detailed study of Goethe's Faust, see E.A. Bucchianeri, *Faust: My Soul be Damned for the World, Vol. 2* (Batalha Publishers: 2010).

emotional conflicts in our daily lives; we may observe our own reflections through this particular story of Faust. It was inevitable composers would be attracted to this legendary classic and be allured by the temptation to set this epic drama to music.

Liszt and the "Faustian Conflict"

Franz Liszt was born in Hungary in 1811 and died at Bayreuth in 1886. He received his first piano lessons from his father, and later studied with Czerny, becoming one of the world's most famous musicians. His skill as a performer astounded audiences, earning him fabulous fortunes from which he gave generously to charity. Upon reaching the pinnacle of his concert career, he renounced it in favour of a court position at Weimar in 1849. He relocated to Rome in 1861, and in 1865, took minor orders of the Church. Perpetually on the move between Weimar, Rome and Budapest, he continued teaching and performing. Apparently, Liszt was in a continual polemic conflict, yearning for a glorious career in the limelight in contrast to his craving for seclusion to allow time for composition. Oswald Barrett ('Batt') describes Liszt as a man who had internal conflicts and a restless nature:

"Two opposing forces were continually at war within him. He revelled in the glamour he created, but when satiated with all this he would shut himself away from the world, full of disgust, the desire to write great works strong upon him. Then his delight in the world's applause would prove too strong; he

69

longed again to see fashionable society at his feet and he would emerge again from his isolation.

In his last years his ranking discontent made him more than ever restless. He travelled incessantly, urged on, it would seem, by a burning desire to make amends, for he gave his services wherever they could be applied to a useful purpose, as he had for long given all his lessons free of charge. He was, at heart, a grand old man, yet ever haunted by the spectre of 'the idle uselessness that frets me'."[78]

Apparently, the conflict Liszt experienced was similar to that of Goethe who "drifted about in all knowledge," it was inevitable Goethe's work would influence him in the course of his career.

In 1830, Berlioz first introduced Liszt to Gerard de Nerval's French translation of the drama before the premiere of the *Symphonie Fantastique*, however, many years passed before Liszt composed the *Faust Symphony*.[79] He had sketched several ideas for the symphony, but his demanding concert career prevented him from developing his inspirations. Ironically, upon his appointment as Kapellmeister in Weimar, he refrained from writing the symphony for five years until 1854 and delayed the premiere until 1857. Did Liszt experience a similar predicament to Goethe who could only take delight in his ideas on the subject, but found it difficult to express them? Liszt may have hesitated to set this work due to his respect for Goethe's literary masterpiece, or, the drama and its

---

[78] Oswald Barrett ('Batt'), 'Liszt the Traveller', Plate 93, ed. Percy A. Scholes, *The Oxford Companion to Music* (Oxford: Oxford University Press, 1942).
[79] Walker, *Weimar Years*, p. 326.

philosophical polemics with the "Faustian Conflict" touched a personal chord and he waited until he felt equal to this monumental task. Liszt once remarked, "Anything connected with Goethe is dangerous for me to handle."[80]

During this period, Liszt was continually exposed to Faustian culture and the shadow of Goethe at Weimar; therefore, we suspect it would have been impossible for him to abandon his earlier plans for the symphony. Liszt was nearing the completion of his first term of employment when the Grand Duke decreed that on August 28, 1849, Weimar would host the centenary celebration of Goethe's birth. Liszt conducted various compositions for the festivities, including excerpts from Schumann's *Scenes from Faust*. Later, Liszt contributed to the creation of the Goethe Foundation, which led to the publication of his brochure *De la fondation — Goethe a Weimar*. In 1850, Gerard de Nerval visited Weimar, and Liszt invited him to remain as his guest; one can easily surmise the main topic of their conversations! Later in 1852, Liszt invited Berlioz to Weimar to conduct his work *The Damnation of Faust*, and he was profoundly impressed by Berlioz's musical adaptation.

In the proceeding year 1853, his patron Prince Carl Friedrich died and Carl Alexander succeeded him. When his new patron informed him that the inauguration was to take place on Goethe's birthday, Liszt stated, "… a significant date if they really wish to keep the meaning." Later, Carl Alexander in a conversation with Liszt paraphrased the famous lines* when Faust attempts to translate the

---

[80]   Ibid. p. 327.
*   'Tis writ, "In the beginning was the Word!"
        I pause, perplex'd! Who now will help afford?
        I cannot the mere Word so highly prize;
        I must translate it otherwise, […]

Bible by remarking, "The Word must now become the Deed," recognising the fact that the culture of the region now rested upon him as the new heir. Finally, in 1854, George Henry Lewes, accompanied by the novelist George Eliot (Mary Ann Evans), visited Weimar for research purposes. Lewes was collecting information for his two-volume biography of Goethe; they had frequent meetings with Liszt and discussed Goethe's life and work, including his place and stature within German literature. On August 10th, the conversation centred on Goethe's *Faust*; Lewes and Eliot directed their questions to Liszt's companion, Princess Carolyne Sayn-Wittgenstein, who dismissed Goethe as an 'egoist'.[81]

With this continual exposure, apparently these latter events proved to be the decisive factor; Liszt's inspiration to create the symphony had finally blossomed. In August 1854, he commenced work on the symphony and succeeded in finishing it at a breakneck speed by October! Despite this prodigious speed of composition, he did not premiere the work immediately. He added the Chorus Mysticus three years later, and the symphony finally premiered on September 5th, 1857 in Weimar. It was performed at a concert in honour of the laying of the foundation stone for the monument dedicated to the Grand Duke Carl August, the patron of Goethe and Schiller; possibly, Liszt decided to add the chorus for this celebration.

In addition, we note there is a marked change in Liszt's productivity in composition and conducting performances dating shortly before the completion of the *Faust Symphony* in 1854, and in

---

I write; "In the beginning was the Deed!"

Faust, Harvard Classics, p. 54.
[81] Walker, *Weimar Years*, p. 327.

the proceeding years. For the first time in 1854, Liszt introduced the term 'symphonic poem' with *Tasso,* which premiered on April 19th of that year. Intriguingly, many of Liszt's symphonic poems were composed, in the process of revision, or performed in or around 1854 to 1857, the years he was occupied with the *Faust Symphony.*[82]

Title	Composition / revision dates	Performance
'on entend sur la montage (After Victor Hugo)	(1) 1848–49, scored by Raff	Weimar, Feb. 1850, under Liszt
	(2) 1850, scored by Raff	Weimar, 1853, under Liszt
	(3) 1854, scored by Liszt	**Weimar, Jan. 7, 1857, under Liszt**
Tasso: Lamento e trionfo (After Byron): **(Term 'Symphonic Poem' first used publicly with this work.)**	(1) 1841–45, Liszt's sketch	
	(2) scored by Conradi, later corrected by Liszt	Weimar, Aug 28, 1849, As overture to Goethe's *Torquato Tasso*
	(3) 1850–51, scored by Raff	
	(4) 1854, revised by Liszt (central section appears for first time)	**Weimar, April 19, 1854, under Liszt**
Les Préludes (After Lamartine)	(1) 1848, as an introduction to the choral	

[82] Symphonic Poem Listing, Walker, *Weimar Years*, pp. 301–302.

	work *Les Quatre Elémens*	
	(2) early 1850s, revised by Liszt	**Weimar, Feb. 23, 1854, under Liszt**
Orpheus	**1853–54**	**Weimar, Feb. 16,1854, as introduction to Gluck's** *Orpheus and Eurydice,* **under Liszt**
Prometheus	(1) 1850, as overture to the choruses from Herder's *Prometheus,* scored by Raff	Weimar, August 24, 1850, under Liszt
	(2) 1855, revised by Liszt	**Braunschweig, Oct. 18, 1855, under Liszt**
Mazeppa (After Victor Hugo, expanded from the piano study)	(1) 1851, scored by Raff	
	(2) 1854, revised by Liszt	**Weimar, April 16, 1854, under Liszt**
Festklänge (Intended for Liszt's forthcoming nuptials with Princess Caroline)	1853	**Weimar Nov. 9, 1854, under Liszt**
Héroïde Funèbre (Based on first movement of early "Revolutionary" Symphony)	(1) 1849–50, scored by Raff **(2) 1854, scored by Liszt**	**Breslau, Nov. 10, 1857**
Hungaria	**1854**	**Pest National Theatre, Sept. 8, 1856, under Liszt**
Hamlet	1858, as prelude to Shakespeare's play	Sondershausen, July 2, 1876, under Max Erdmannsdörfer
Hunnenschlacht (After Kaulbach)	**1857**	**Weimar, Dec. 29, 1857, under Liszt**

Die Ideale (After Schiller)	1857	Weimar, Sept. 5, 1857, Under Liszt
❧✦❧	SYMPHONIES	❧✦❧
Faust Symphony, in *three character sketches* (After Goethe)	(1) 1854 (2) 1857, addition of final chorus	Weimar, Sept. 5, under Liszt
Dante Symphony	1855–56	Dresden, Nov. 7, 1857, Under Liszt

Is it possible Liszt was inspired to create the symphonic poem genre due to his interest in Goethe's *Faust?* Goethe introduces his drama with two prologues, the Prologue for the Theatre, and the Prologue in Heaven. The first prologue presents three characters, the Theatre Manager, the Merryman and a Poet who describes and explains the nature of the drama to be performed. The Manager and the Merryman wish to produce a work pleasing to the general populace in an attempt to fill the theatre, yet the Poet refuses to partake in this endeavour as it does not aspire to his high ambitions in art. The Manager and the Merryman agree that the Poet may present a drama he considers sophisticated, as they are curious to discover his interpretation of a 'noble' production. Apparently, Goethe wished to reform German culture by directing his readers to meditate on issues he considered 'intellectual' and therefore 'noble'. This element of *Faust* may have appealed to Liszt. The Theatre Manager is willing to present un-intellectual entertainments for increased ticket sales; in 1853, Liszt once remarked in a soured tone that everyone in Weimar had a box-office mentality and that ticket-sales were then the primary issue as plays were more popular than concerts.[83] Walker diligently relates Liszt was determined to re-establish Weimar as a great cultural centre, yet his ambitions were thwarted for several reasons. Many of Liszt's ideas were too idealistic and not readily feasible, and he had difficulty with obtaining funds due to the 'tight-fisted' tendencies of his patron Carl Alexander. The orchestra lacked a significant number of professional musicians and the standard expected by Liszt was not always maintained. In addition, Liszt was forced to endure local opposition due to the provincial mentality of many citizens who viewed him as a 'worldly' foreigner invading their town.

Possibly, the musical aspect of the two Prologues also attracted Liszt; in the Theatre Prologue, the Poet continually refers to music when describing his own lofty ideals, dismissing less intellectual works with lines that read:

> No, to some peaceful heavenly nook restore me,
> Where only for the bard blooms pure delight, [...]
>
> What! Shall the bard his godlike power abuse? [...]
>
> But from the harmony that gushing from his soul,
> Draws back into his heart the wondrous whole? [...]
>
> In rhythmic flow to music's measur'd tone?
> Each solitary note whose genius calleth,
> To swell the mighty choir in unison? [...]

---

[83] Walker, *Weimar Years*, p. 135.

Man's mighty spirit, in the bard reveal'd!

In the next scene, the Prologue in Heaven, the link continues between music and all that is 'noble' and awe-inspiring. The first elements of Creation praised by the Archangel Raphael are the sun and the spheres, the spheres in rival song. Here, Goethe was referring to the Medieval theory regarding the 'music of the spheres'; it was believed that the planets emitted a celestial tone as they revolved in the heavens. Later, this term survived in poetic language. We observe with these two prologues the gradual erasing of boundaries between the arts, an important concept during the Romantic Era. Apparently, Liszt became inspired by Goethe's attempt to describe the lofty career of a poet with musical references. If the poet, linked to the noble properties of the mind is associated with the realm of music, naturally it follows that music, often considered the noblest of the arts, would most assuredly be correlated with literature. Liszt defended the concept of the symphonic poem by writing:

> "From time immemorial the sung word has occasioned or developed a connection between music and literary or quasi-literary works. The present attempt, however, is intended as a fusion of the two, which promises to become more intimate than heretofore achieved. More and more the masterpieces of music will absorb the masterpieces of literature. [...] On what grounds should music, which was so inseparably associated with Sophocle's tragedies and

Pindar's odes, hesitate at the thought of becoming fused — differently, but yet more fittingly — with literary works of post-Classical inspiration, of becoming identified with names such as Dante and Shakespeare?"[84]

Goethe's philosophical concepts portrayed in Faust possibly fuelled Liszt's ambition to raise the cultural standards in Weimar, and thus contributed to the conception of the symphonic poem.

Liszt and *Faust,* Symphonic Poem or Symphony?

When Liszt commenced the development of the *Faust Symphony,* he was entering a polemic battlefield. During the Romantic Era, many believed that music was the only medium capable of true emotional expression. Alfred Einstein states, "Music became a medium through which the ineffable could be palpable to sense, through which the mysterious, magical, and exciting could be created."[85] Instrumental music gained supremacy due to the admiration of Beethoven's compositions as Einstein relates:

> "Beethoven was above all the creator and perfecter of the symphony, the sonata, and the quartet, ...
> The reason that Beethoven, with his instrumental inclinations, became so influential a

---

[84] Alfred Einstein, *Music in the Romantic Era* (London, J. M. Dent and Sons, Ltd.:1947), p. 24. *Gesammelte Schriften* (Leipzig, 1882), IV, p. 58 f.
[85] Ibid. p. 21.

model lies in the fact that the Romantics saw something different in the symphonic, in chamber music, in *wordless* music, than did the preceding generation. ... It became the choicest means of saying what could not be said, of expressing something deeper than the *word* had been able to express. ... .

... And it was due to a characteristic misunderstanding by the Romantics that they admired his symphonies not because of the definiteness and clearness of the form, the taming of all the chaotic impulses, but because of the manifold possibility of interpreting them. ... Thus, to the Romantics, instrumental music appeared also a manifestation of the mystical."[86]

Due to this perception, many Romantic composers desired to continue the symphonic tradition after Beethoven, however, the drive to compose works that were unique and original proved to be almost impossible. Many composers found the task to compose unique symphonies too difficult while the shadow of Beethoven loomed as an obstacle ever before them. The return to program music with its roots planted in literature became the solution for many of the Romantic composers, however, critics argued that only absolute music without programmatic content was capable of definite emotional and spiritual expression. Arthur Schopenhauer maintained that music should exist completely independent of text as

---

[86] Ibid. pp. 32–33.

words were of "secondary value."[87]   Eduard Hanslick wrote, "The union with poetry, extends the power of music, but not its boundaries."[88]

Apparently, Liszt's tactical defence to the polemical debate was to create a new, and therefore original genre associated with the poetic ideal of expressing emotions while using instrumental forces employed for a symphony. Generally, the symphonic poem consists of a single movement and has a programmatic title based on a poem or literary work, in some instances, the symphonic poem will also have a written programme. This form attracted controversy due to its literary associations, however, several of Beethoven's symphonies such as the "Eroica," the "Pastoral," and the Ninth allude to extra-musical associations, and therefore the programmatic nature of the symphonic poem may also be defended.

It may be questioned why Liszt would choose to set *Faust* as a symphony if Goethe's work inspired his creation of the symphonic poem. One would expect this drama to be the first composition in this new genre as a demonstration of his inspiration; however, on further inspection of the symphony we may perceive Liszt had developed the concept of the symphonic poem to epic proportions.

Intriguingly, Liszt entitles the composition, "A Faust Symphony in Three Character Studies after Goethe." The fact he composed it as a symphony implies an attempt to continue the symphonic tradition of Beethoven, especially with the addition of the Chorus Mysticus that is reminiscent of the Ninth Choral Symphony.

---

[87]   Ibid. p. 340. Arthur Schopenhauer, *The World as Will and Idea* (1st ed. 1818, 2nd ed. 1844).
[88]   Ibid. p. 351. Eduard Hanslick, *On the Beautiful in Music: A Contribution to the Revisal of Musical Aesthetics* (1854).

The characters from Goethe's drama, Faust, Gretchen, and Mephistopheles are allocated a movement in that order; as this symphony is intended as a 'character study', each movement musically explores the various emotional experiences of the characters. We may argue this work could bear no relation to a symphonic poem as this description of the work apparently conforms to a majority of the ideals championed by "Absolute" music supporters. Yet, we cannot ignore the extra-musical associations connected with the composition, it is foremost a programmatic work. In addition, the various themes Liszt uses to portray diverse character emotions occur in sequence with the basic outline of Goethe's drama. Faust's movement contains themes representing Mephistopheles, Gretchen's movement contains several of Faust's themes, while the Mephistopheles movement contains very few new motifs for he parodies most of Faust's themes, in contrast to Gretchen's motifs that remain unblemished by the fiend. Subsequently, it is evident the emotions of each character also portray action and consequential reactions; a story is unfolding, thus we have a positive link with the symphonic poem. Let us briefly examine Liszt's treatment of the themes allocated to each character.

Faust is assigned five different motifs; he has more themes than the other characters for he is forever in turmoil. Liszt stated, "Faust's personality scatters and dissipates himself, he takes no action, lets himself be driven, hesitates, experiments, loses his way, considers, bargains, and is interested in his own little happiness."[89] Nowhere is this more apparent than in the first theme which opens the Slow introduction; this displays one of the first twelve-tone rows

[89] H. Searle, Record notes, 'A Faust Symphony and Symphonic Poem, 'Orpheus'' (Hayes, Middlesex, England: E.M.I. Records Ltd., 1959).

composed in musical history.[90] As it is a chromatic tone row, the key is ambiguous and is not 'stable'. In addition, Vazonyi notes that this tone row consists of four augmented fifth triads, thus the harmony can modulate in any direction.[91] Therefore, this theme aptly portrays Faust's 'lost' and 'endless searching' character. The second theme at Bar 4 perpetuates this characterisation for it contains a falling seventh that misses the octave and the rising response just misses the seventh, thus a sense of resolution is avoided.[92] This may represent Faust's constant striving without reaching a satisfactory conclusion. The sparse orchestration contributes to the poignant aspect of these themes; the first theme is scored exclusively in the subdued string section and the second in the woodwinds with the muted first violins. These themes may represent Faust in the solitude of his study pondering the mysteries of life and his deep despair upon his realisation the earthly knowledge he gained was futile to obtain the happiness he seeks — he had squandered a lifetime in vain pursuit.

Subsequently, the exposition at Bar 23 is introduced with a 'mischievous' new motif that alters the ambience created in the Slow introduction. The tempo is marked *Allegro impetuoso*, the dynamic sound is *forte*, and the strings section is not muted. The first and second violins present the semiquaver motif consisting of an augmented fourth from B to F; hence, we may observe the 'diabolus in musica' — the 'devil in music' has responded to Faust's augmented fifths. Faust apparently replies for his first theme is restated in Bar 45, and his second theme repeated in Bar 66 is reorchestrated as a 'dark' bassoon solo; perhaps Faust is considering Mephistopheles'

---

[90]   Walker, *Weimar Years*, p. 329.
[91]   Vazonyi, 'List, Goethe, Faust Symphony', p. 4.
[92]   Ibid.

offer and has reached a decision? At Bar 71, Faust's third theme is introduced in the string section that may signify the signing of the contract, and a new fourth theme at Bar112 featuring *tremolo* strings which could indicate Faust's transformation; he has been granted the restoration of youth. Later in the exposition, Faust's second theme returns at Bar 179 and has been re-orchestrated for the clarinets, bassoon, horns, and the 'mellow' section of the strings i.e. the violas and 'cellos. The tempo is marked *Affettuoso poco Andante* and the overall dynamic is *piano*. Faust's second theme thereby assumes an 'amorous' quintessence suggesting he has encountered Gretchen. Faust's fifth and final theme at Bar 225 is introduced with an orchestral *tutti*. This new theme resembles a militaristic fanfare; it is in the bright key of E major and is 'heroic' in style. Faust may have concluded his quest for true happiness would be realised with his conquest of Gretchen's affections; perhaps at this point Faust demands that Mephistopheles assist him with his courtship of Gretchen. In summary, we may observe there is evidence of a continual development of the dramatic plot in Faust's movement.

The drama continues to unfold in Gretchen's movement. Gretchen has been assigned only two themes in contrast to the tumultuous nature of Faust's character. Her first theme commences at Bar 15 with a quiet melodic passage played by the oboes, and violas; the tempo is *Andante soave*. Intriguingly, Faust's second theme is introduced as a descending scale at Bar 45 with the oboes, which is immediately proceeded at Bar 51 with a section depicting Gretchen plucking the petals of a daisy; 'he loves me, he loves me not'. Therefore, we are aware Gretchen has encountered Faust, and is thinking of him. Liszt incorporates a hemiola by crossing compound quadruple 12/8 time with simple quadruple 4/4 time; this is one of the few musical sections which depicts action rather than simply evoke an emotion. Succeeding this section, Gretchen's first theme is heard at Bar 57, and her new second theme is introduced at Bar 83 by the string section. In the development area commencing at Bar 112, Faust's second and third themes are predominant suggesting he is physically present. This interpretation is confirmed within the recapitulation beginning at Bar 204; the 'Flower Petal' scene does not return indicating she is no longer daydreaming as he is there in person. Faust's fifth 'heroic' theme introduced near the conclusion of her movement suggests he has succeeded in winning Gretchen's affections.

The interaction between the various themes continues with the Mephistopheles movement; as mentioned, a considerable number of the devil's themes are parodies of Faust's motifs. This not only signifies the manipulative power in which he holds Faust; he is also a dark spirit of negation who despite his own power cannot create and is only capable of destroying the good that surrounds him. The destructive power of the devil is demonstrated proficiently by the nature of his two themes that are independent of those associated with Faust. The first theme is the 'Mischievous' motif which was introduced at Bar 23 of the first movement when the devil tempted Faust; it commences the third movement and has been developed into a septuplet chromatic scale. The second motif at Bar 47 is a new theme Liszt borrowed from a separate work he composed for piano and strings entitled "Malediction."[93] The statement of these themes in

---

[93] H. Searle, Record notes.

the exposition may represent Mephistopheles entertaining Faust at the Walpurgis Night orgy. In the development section at Bar 157, Faust's second theme is introduced as a fugal passage in the string section followed by the 'heroic' fifth theme at Bar 246; this may symbolise Faust demanding the devil to rescue Gretchen from prison. Gretchen's theme concludes the development section and has not been parodied; the devil cannot obtain dominion over her as she turns to God for forgiveness. Liszt initially intended the movement to conclude with a 'melting climax' that portrayed Faust's soul elevated by angels to Heaven on Gretchen's theme; notice the rising triplet crotchets in the woodwind section followed by the section marked *Poco Andante, ma sempre all breve*.[94] Apparently, Liszt endeavoured to portray the drama of Goethe's *Faust* through his music in addition to his musical exploration of their emotions.

Interestingly, if we eliminate the title of each movement the composition assumes the aspect of a one-movement work. The "Faust" and "Mephistopheles" sections may act as the exposition and recapitulation of sonata form, as the "Mephistopheles" movement is a large parody of the "Faust" movement, and the second movement thereby acts as a development section. Was Liszt attempting to compose an epic symphonic poem? One may argue Liszt had defeated this purpose by adding the Chorus Mysticus as the sung text contradicts the instrumental nature of a symphonic poem, and appears as an imitation of Beethoven's Ninth symphony thus undermining the concept of originality. However, we must not overlook the fact he completed the symphony without the chorus and it was sufficient unto itself.

---

[94] Walker, *Weimar Years*, p. 334.

Why did Liszt decide to add the text three years later if the original Coda adequately represented Faust's salvation? Perhaps the remark his patron Carl Alexander made to him in 1853 may shed some light, "The Word must now become the Deed." As mentioned, his patron was referring to Faust's translation of St. John's Gospel in the Bible. Faust adapts the sacred text by changing "In the beginning was the Word" to "In the beginning was the Deed." Perchance this symbolises the accomplishment of God's promise of salvation. God is the "Word" who willed our salvation, became incarnate and by His death consummated the fulfilment of His promise; is this not the ultimate Deed? Liszt, who was a profoundly religious man, may have regarded this symbolism extremely important. In the symphony, the sung text of the Chorus Mysticus may reflect the concept of the word becoming the deed. The chorus intone the last lines of Goethe's *Faust* Part II symbolising salvation for mankind:

> All that is past of us
> Was but reflected;
> All that was lost in us
> Here is corrected;
> All indescribables
> Here we descry
> The Eternal Feminine
> Leads us on High.

In effect, Liszt had composed the symphony with a dual inference; initially he created an epic symphonic poem, and with the addition of the chorus, a poetic symphony. Thereby, he merged the controversial symphonic poem genre, with the 'noble' and admired characteristics of a Beethoven symphony, validating the concept that the boundaries between music and literature could be effectively eradicated. The "Word" could become the "Deed" through the art of music.

❧ ♦ ❧

Orientalism, Music, and Debussy:
West Meets East

For centuries, Europeans erected an invisible barrier between the West and the East supported by the academic field of Orientalism. The intended purpose of this branch of study was to collect information and obtain knowledge of the Orient; later Western countries used this acquired knowledge to aid in colonization campaigns and facilitate the occupation and management of countries considered inferior to Western culture. The generally accepted concept was the greater the knowledge, the greater the power and control that could be exerted over nations classified as primitive.[95] The West viewed the East as a dark, mysterious, and barbaric world due to its various pagan customs and seemingly 'backward' governmental systems. Gradually, Orientalism influenced the public's imagination and the world of art, music and literature; although, it is difficult to imagine the ethereal art of music could be susceptible to the darker aspects of human nature such as stereotyping, prejudicial labelling and racism.

Due to Orientalism, composers depicted the East as comical, or a land of fantasy; the East was romanticised as a region shrouded by the ambience of the fantastic and mystique, thus becoming the land of dreams and fairytales. In essence, music influenced by Orientalism in the Romantic Era exemplifies how the West viewed

---

[95] Edward W. Said, *Orientalism* (England: Pantheon Books, St. Ives plc., 1978), p. 36.

the East with the implementation of stylistic devices rather than experimentation with Eastern musical traditions for the purpose of cultural exchange. In contrast to this prejudicial outlook, Claude Debussy was one of the first influential Western composers to display a genuine interest in the Javanese Gamelan, the orchestra of Java, and believed Western music could benefit from the study of Javanese tradition.[96] In the course of this essay, we will explore the development of Orientalism and examine its influence and effects on Western music, including Debussy's avant-garde approach and interpretations.

Orientalism originally immerged from fear of the unknown and the threat of invasion. After Mohammed's death in 632, the religion and culture of Islam rapidly disseminated through military occupation. Muslim invaders first captured Persia, Syria, Egypt, Turkey and North Africa. During the eighth and ninth centuries, their conquests extended to Spain, Sicily and regions of France, and by the thirteenth and fourteenth centuries, India, Indonesia and China fell under Islamic rule. European countries were alarmed at the expansion of Islam; this religion and its culture symbolised terror and destruction by pagan barbaric armies and Europeans regarded this fearful situation with awe. Until the end of the seventeenth century, this fear of danger lurked ominously close to European borders in the form of the Ottoman Empire.[97] According to European schools of thought, the acquisition of knowledge became vital for the survival of Christian Europe. This quest for knowledge commenced with the Church Council of Vienne in 1312 which established a series of chairs in Arabic, Greek, Hebrew and Syriac in places of

---

[96] Neil Sorrel, *A Guide to the Gamelan* (London: Faber and Faber Ltd., 1990), p. 2.
[97] Said, *Orientalism*, p. 59.

academic learning such as Paris, Oxford, Bologna, Avignon and Salamanca.[98]

During the Middle Ages and the early Renaissance period, a savage portrayal of Islam became intensified through a variety of mediums such as poetry, general superstition and prejudice. By the middle of the fifteenth century, Europeans reached a consensus that action was obviously necessary to oppose this threat. In 1450–1460, Aeneas Silvius (Pope Pius II), John of Segovia, Nicholas of Cusa, and Jean Germain held a conference to determine a possible solution; although they failed to reach an agreement, Edward Said states this conference exemplifies a major attempt to contrast the Orient with European culture.[99]

From the seventeenth century, the acquisition of knowledge concerning the Orient became primarily the task of the Orientalists, who thereby influenced European perceptions of the East with their writings. To all intents and purposes, the Orientalists were propagandists; their information was not always truthful, accurate, or factual as they utilised superstition and myth to present their findings. Hence, the knowledge that the Europeans gained and accepted of the Orient was either half-truth or imaginative documentation. A prime example of this misrepresentation of the East is prefigured with Barthelemy d'Herbelot's posthumously published work *Bibliotheque Oriental* (1697). With the exception of Johann H. Hottinger's book *Historia Orientalis* (1651), the *Bibliotheque* remained the established official reference book concerning Oriental culture in Europe until the early nineteenth

---

[98] Ibid. pp. 49–50.
[99] Ibid. p. 61.

century.[100]   Ironically, d'Herbelot did not attempt to correct the commonly held beliefs and misconceptions concerning the East; he merely listed all previously known places, names, and vague histories of Levantine and Islamic culture in alphabetical order, and in doing so endorsed the false impressions entertained by Europeans as factual information.   This work set the precedence for future Orientalists; their task was to confirm the accepted stereotyping of Western superiority rather than present truthful and unbiased accounts. Finally, the field of Orientalism became firmly established; in an attempt to understand the Orient, Europeans referenced their information from the work of the 'knowledgeable' Orientalists as Westerners did not refer to the original Oriental sources but preferred to depend on the misinformation offered by these accepted academic experts.[101]

During the nineteenth century, Orientalism blossomed resulting from the various colonial wars fought between England and France, particularly with Napoleon's campaigns.   The Orient attracted Napoleon in his youth; his early writings contain a summary of Marigny's *History of the Arabs*, and he wrote of the past glories of Alexander the Great, paying particular attention to the conquest of Egypt.   Apparently, the dream to reconquer Egypt as a new Alexander proved tempting, particularly when this campaign would afford him the opportunity to strategically acquire a colony at the expense of England; Egypt was the gateway to the British Oriental Empire.[102]   As a requisite to carry out this strategy, Napoleon

---

[100]   Ibid. p. 65.
[101]   Ibid. pp. 66–67.
[102]   Ibid. pp. 76, 80.

gathered the necessary intelligence concerning Egypt and the Orient, and in doing so, relied on the expertise of the Orientalists.

Napoleon acquired his knowledge of Egypt from Comte de Volney's book *Voyage en Egypte et en Syrie*, and subsequently commissioned two research projects. The first commission was assigned to Abraham-Hyacinthe Anquetil-Duperron (1731–1805) who was despatched to India to translate Avestan texts. A new awareness of Oriental culture surfaced due to newly discovered texts in Arabic, Sanskrit, and Zend that were then translated; discoveries attributed to Napoleon's colonisation projects.[103] For the first time Europe was afforded an opportunity to view the East through accurate accounts of its civilisations and languages from original texts. An intellectual and historical quality of Orientalism was presented to Europe, which helped to dispel some misconceptions of Asia and its geographical dimensions. The second commission was assigned to William Jones; unfortunately, Jones narrowed the horizons of Orientalism and neutralised Anquetil-Duperron's progressive work. Jones' objective was to codify and tabulate the knowledge he acquired in an effort to suppress the various Oriental cultures into a complete digest of works, customs, laws and figures.[104] This retrogression is similar to d'Herbelot's alphabetical work published in the *Bibliotheque*. In summary, Napoleon initially obtained his knowledge of Egypt from Orientalist research and not from personal experience; he perceived the Orient primarily from classical texts and the opinions of Orientalist experts. This is the first instance where Orientalism was deployed for colonial purposes.[105]

---

[103] Ibid. p. 42.
[104] Ibid. pp. 77–78.
[105] Ibid. p. 80.

From the 1870s, Orientalism flourished and gradually assumed an ominous perspective. The West now regarded the East in terms similar to Darwinism; Oriental races were categorised as inferior and primitive in contrast to Western cultures considered superior and civilised. Orientals at that time were conveniently perceived to have considerable mental and physical inadequacies, and were contrasted with Europeans in an effort to prove the superiority and progressive nature of Western civilisation. Lord Evelyn Baring Cromer, the British representative stationed in Egypt from 1882 to 1907, wrote this bigoted statement in the thirty-fourth chapter of his two-volume work *Modern Egypt*:

> "Sir Alfred Lyall once said to me; 'Accuracy is abhorrent to the Oriental mind. Every Anglo-Indian should always remember that maxim.' Want of accuracy, which easily degenerates into untruthfulness, is in fact the main characteristic of the Oriental mind.
>
> The European is a close reasoner; his statements of fact are devoid of any ambiguity; he is a natural logician, albeit he may not have studied logic; he is by nature sceptical and requires proof before he can accept the truth of any proposition; his trained intelligence works like a piece of mechanism. The mind of the Oriental, on the other hand, like his picturesque streets, is eminently wanting in symmetry. His reasoning is of the most slipshod description. Although the Arabs acquired in a

somewhat higher degree the science of dialectics, their descendants are singularly deficient in the logical faculty. They are often incapable of drawing the most obvious conclusions from any simple premises of which they may admit the truth. Endeavour to elicit a plain statement of facts from any ordinary Egyptian. His explanation will generally be lengthy, and wanting in lucidity. He will probably contradict himself half a dozen times before he has finished his story. He will often break down under the mildest process of cross-examination."[106]

In the nineteenth century, this distorted development of Orientalism was perpetuated essentially to justify European Imperialism.[107] Subject races considered primitive and 'simple' were deemed incapable of self-government.[108] Therefore, it would be at the discretion of the European 'superior intellect' to point the way by means of colonisation as Arthur J. Balfour stated when addressing the House of Commons in 1910 concerning the British occupation of Egypt:

"First of all, look at the facts of the case. Western nations as soon as they emerge into history show the beginnings of those capacities of self-government ... having merits of their own. ... You may look through the whole history of the Orientals

---

[106]   Ibid. p. 38.
[107]   Dr. Michael Murphy, *Lecture*, November 6, 1997. Also, *Orientalism*, p. 206.
[108]   Ibid. p. 37.

in what is called, broadly speaking, the East, and you never find traces of self-government. All their great centuries — and they have been very great — have passed under despotisms, under absolute government. All their great contributions to civilisation — and they have been great — have been under that form of government. Conqueror has succeeded conqueror; one domination has followed another; but never in all the revolutions of fate and fortune have you seen one of those nations of its own motion establish what we, from a Western point of view, call self-government.

...

It is a good thing for these great nations — I admit their greatness — that this absolute government should be exercised by us? I think it is a good thing. I think that experience shows that they have got under it far better government than in the whole history of the world they ever new before, and which is not only a benefit to them, but is undoubtedly a benefit to the whole of the civilised West. ... We are in Egypt not merely for the sake of Egyptians, though we are there for their sake; we are there also for the sake of Europe at large."[109]

Interestingly, as the European individual was proclaimed the superior being, he was made to appear so in the eyes of the subjected races; the Oriental was never to observe a Westerner becoming aged

---

[109] Ibid. pp. 32–33.

or degenerate, thus it became common practise in the British colonies to retire their administrators before they reached the age of fifty-five.[110]

In summary, the Orientalists painted the picture of the Orient and presented it to Europe; they were the learned academics who studied the various languages and customs of the Oriental races and were therefore trusted sources and their expertise was relied upon on matters concerning the Orient.[111] Europeans obtained their information of the Oriental civilisations through the Western propaganda of the Orientalists. Therefore, when referring to the early academic field of Orientalism, we are not relating to a study of the actual historical facts of Eastern cultures, but rather a stereotyped perception of the East from a biased Western viewpoint.

It is hardly surprising to discover Orientalism influencing music of the Romantic Era; both share a common background. After the French Revolution, the rise of Napoleon and his campaigns contributed immensely to the growth of Orientalism, hence Paris became the capital of this academic branch. Paris also became the new musical capital of Europe after the Revolution; the weight of musical patronage transferred from the Church and the aristocracy to the middle classes, heralding the change in concert venues from concert halls to the private salons and the emergence of new styles and genres. The waltz replaced the aristocratic minuet as the popular dance of the people, and the piano became the predominant instrument for salon entertainments with its own unique genres such as nocturnes, ballads, etudes, and virtuoso showpieces.[112] Due to the

---

[110] Ibid. p. 42.
[111] Ibid. p. 67.
[112] Dr. Murphy, *Lecture*, October 17, 1997.

close proximity between the arts and the political environment within the same capital, an association naturally immerged between Romanticism and the concept of Orientalism.[113] The Orientalist Friedrich Schlegel said in 1800, "It is in the Orient that we must search for the highest Romanticism."[114] Novelists, poets, artists and musicians created many works depicting the Orient as a sensual and dangerous realm reflecting the vogue for Orientalism.[115] The English poet Lord Byron, considered one of the defining poets of Romanticism, on occasions dressed in Albanian costumes — thus displaying his fascination with the Orient![116] Victor Hugo wrote in his preface to *Les Orientals* (1829), "In the age of Louis the XIV one was a Hellenist, today, one is an Orientalist. The entire continent is leaning towards the Orient."[117] The preoccupation of Romantic idealists to travel and explore far off and exotic countries was also an important venture for the Orientalists. Several musicians travelled to the Orient, it was inevitable that music would assimilate Orientalist idealism. E.T.A. Hoffmann believed that music portrayed a:

> " ... faraway country which surrounds us often with the strangest presentiments and from which wondrous voices call down to us, wakening all the echoes that sleep in our restricted breasts, which echoes awakening now, shoot joyfully and gladly up, as though fiery rays, making us sharers in the bliss of

---

[113] Alfred Einstein, *Music in the Romantic Era* (U.S.A.: J.M. Dent and Sons, Ltd., 1947), p. 57.
[114] Said, *Orientalism*, p. 98.
[115] Dr. Murphy, *Lecture*, November 6, 1997. Also, *Orientalism*, p. 118.
[116] Dr. Murphy, ibid.
[117] Ibid. Lecture, October 23, 1997. Also, *Orientalism*, p. 51.

that paradise. ... Is not music the mysterious language of a faraway spirit world whose wondrous accents, echoing within us, awaken us to a higher, more intense life? All the passions battle with one another, their armour shimmering and sparkling, perishing in an inexpressible yearning which fills our breasts."

Western musicians composed their "Oriental" music in true Orientalist fashion; they depicted the Occidental perception of the East through music. Due to the programmatic element in music and the use of orchestral 'tone colouring' it was common practise to paint 'musical pictures' portraying the East. Maurice Ravel's *Sheherazade* is an example of this style of composition depicting the West's fascination with the East through Western orchestral instrumentation. Ravel set three poems written by Arthur Justin Leclere, (alias Tristan Klingsor); these poems aptly demonstrate what is termed the 'Oriental Gaze', i.e. the West dreaming and contemplating the mysteries of the Orient. The first poem entitled *Asia* features a Westerner who relates his fantasised perception of the Orient and desires to see the mystical marvels of the East:

> Asia, Asia, Asia,
> Old wonderland of nursery tales
> Where fantasy sleeps like an empress
> In her forest full of mystery. ...
>
> I should like to see Persia, and India, and then China,
> Portly mandarins under parasols

And the princesses with their slender hands,
And the scholars disputing
On poetry and beauty, [...]

As mentioned previously, the Orient was perceived as savage and barbaric. This is also depicted in the first poem, *Asia*.

  I should like to see assassins smile
As the executioner strikes an innocent's neck
With his great curved oriental sword.
I should like to see the poor and queens,
I should like to see roses and blood,
I should like to see death from love or from hate, [...]

The second poem, *The Enchanted Flute*, depicts an Oriental servant girl listening to her sweetheart who plays his flute in the mysterious Oriental night:

The shadow is soft and my master sleeps,
A cone-shaped silken cap upon his head
And his long, yellow nose in his white beard.
But I, I am still awake
And I hear outside
the song of a flute pouring out
sadness or joy, turn by turn —
an air that, now languid now flighty,
my dear sweetheart plays, [...]

The third poem, entitled *The Indifferent One*, exemplifies the author's fascination with the captivating nature of the Orientals through his Romanticised description of a young Oriental stranger as he passes by:

> Your eyes are soft like those of a girl. […]

> But no, you pass,
> And from my threshold I see you move on
> Making me a parting gesture full of grace,
> your hip lightly inclined
> by your girlish, languid gait. […]

These poems illustrate the fantasised stereotyping by Westerners of the Orient, particularly during the nineteenth century; the Orient was a wonderland full of adventure, yet considered elusive and 'mysterious' as a woman. Note the line in the first poem, "Where fantasy sleeps like an empress." The West frequently feminised the Orient; Western civilisation was considered the 'real' and intellectual world, the masculine element, while the Orient represented the passive, passionate feminine element.

Leclere's text depicts the East in a dream-like state, Ravel accordingly sets it in a similar fashion just as 'vague' as the West's perception of the Orient. He uses tonal dissonances that do not resolve into typical perfect cadences, the music remains 'aloof' and 'dreamy'. With his orchestration he created 'rich', blurred sonorities, the melodic phrases flow continually, producing a near hypnotic and mesmerising effect similar to an Eastern mantra. Ravel's *Sheherazade* is an excellent example of musical Orientalism.

When attempting to define Orientalism in music, we encounter an issue that is difficult to resolve; how may we recognise the defining line between Orientalism and exoticism in music? Compositions similar to Ravel's *Sheherazade* have initiated countless debates concerning this particular subject. Perhaps we may observe that a composition tinged with exoticism need not necessarily be Orientalist, while compositions in the realm of Orientalism are by nature exotic works. Orientalism in the nineteenth century was essentially the product of eighteenth century exoticism, [118] and during the eighteenth century, composers such as Mozart employed settings of the Orient for exotic effect.[119] As observed in his opera *Cossi Fan Tutte*, Mozart depicted Orientals as comical characters for exotic purposes, and did not necessarily portray authentic Orientalism. Later in the nineteenth century, Beethoven was one of the first composers to herald a serious application of Orientalism in music as he introduced a Turkish March in his Ninth Symphony. He was audacious in his use of this March for he juxtaposed this 'non-serious' element with the revered style of Western fugal composition, and thereby displayed Orientalism and exoticism simultaneously. Although Beethoven was not depicting the Orient as a musical picture as observed in Ravel's work, he appears to have included the Orient and its people on a universal level by equally addressing all of mankind through his setting of Schiller's Ode. In this symphony, Beethoven assumed a serious attitude concerning the Orient in contrast to the comical perception of the East generally accepted in

---

[118] Dr. Murphy, *Lecture*, October 23, 1997.
[119] Said, *Orientalism*, p. 118.

101

the seventeenth and eighteenth centuries, and in the process had included an exotic element. With Ravel's musical illustration of the "Oriental Gaze" in *Sheherazade*, his work emanates an exotic ambience due to his Oriental subject and orchestral approach. Gustav Holst's *Oriental Suite, Beni Mora*, Op. 29 may also be considered Oriental in nature and therefore exotic; Holst borrowed an authentic Albanian motif and structured his composition upon the 'changing background' technique where a melody is repeated by continuously varying the orchestration thus avoiding aural monotony.

Examples of 'simple' exoticism, i.e. exoticism without the use of Orientalism, are discernable in the Romantic vogue for folk songs from nations other than those adopted from the Orient. For instance, Chopin's *Fanatsie on Polish Folk Songs* Op. 13 would have been considered exotic and unique to the people of France as his work featured songs foreign to French culture. Other composers wrote in a pastiche style as a reference to exotic, foreign cultures; Ravel composed an opera entitled *Spanish Hour* and composed the music to reflect a Spanish style, hence, the opera would sound exotic to French audiences. The French opera *Carmen* is also a prime example; the French composer Bizet wrote this opera in a Spanish Gypsy pastiche style — the famous 'Habanera' is not a Spanish folk song, but we are content to be aurally persuaded by its Cuban rhythmic pulse. The Russian composer Rimsky Korsakov composed a work entitled *Capriccio Espanol* also reflecting this exotic trend.

We should note that during this time, Orientalism and exoticism in music did not necessarily signify the reproduction of authentic Oriental and foreign musical tradition. In contrast, composers endeavoured to produce *authentic sounding* music. For instance, we may argue that if Beethoven intended to compose an *authentic* Turkish march for the Ninth Symphony, he would have been required to research the fundamentals of traditional Turkish music, resulting with a march composed in an authentic style with the use of traditional Turkish instruments. In contrast, Beethoven's march was *authentic sounding* to contemporary European audiences due to the inclusion of Janissary instruments, i.e., 'Jingling Johnnies' in his orchestration. We may apply the same observation to Ravel and Rimsky Korsakov's versions of *Sheherazade*, both composers orchestrated these compositions for a Western orchestra, they did not travel to Asia and study traditional Oriental music. With regard to 'exotic' compositions, composers employed a 'flavouring technique' to give a semblance of authenticity to their works. Korsakov used a C-sharp / C-natural motif in his *Capriccio Espanol* to produce a 'Spanish flavour'. Ravel employed a motif consisting of an augmented second in his composition *Tzigane (Gypsy)* to imbue his music with the essence of traditional Gypsy music.

Exoticism also fell prey to mercenary opportunism. Frequently compositions received misleading titles, deployed as an effective marketing strategy. We may observe an extreme case of misrepresentation with Glasounov's *Finnish Fantasia* Op. 88; the composition was not derived from Finnish folk songs, but from a Lutheran choral, *Einfesteburg*! Glasounov was credited with having a vast knowledge of folk songs, therefore people assumed the composition was based on traditional Finnish music as the title claimed.[120] Music publishers frequently assigned false titles as the demand for exotic music was at a premium.

Orientalism and exoticism in music also had its considerable share of critics. C. Hubert H. Parry, former director of the Royal College of Music in London, ridiculed this fashionable development in music in his publication *Style in Musical Art* (1911). He prejudicially argued that orchestration involving 'tone colouring' and musical repetition of phrases was similar to the 'primitive' music of the 'un-intellectual' Orientals:

> "Another side of the effect on human beings of living indolently indulgent lives [i.e. the Orientals] is the development of abnormal susceptibility. It is the inevitable result of excluding the intellectual. The human being of that type become specially susceptible to colour and quality of tone. To enjoy thrills of sensibility derived from very subtle effects of sound such as are now universally classed as colour effects, requires no energy or exercise of mind or body. It merely requires the creature to be receptive. ... The veneer which just glosses over the elemental savage is so thin that it is often easy to see through it in music as much as in social conditions. ... The unmitigated savage loves to be excited by colour and also by sheer uproar. ...

---

[120] Dr. Murphy, *Lecture*, November 20, 1997.

Almost simultaneously with the conspicuous appearance in art of features which imply a relaxation of the powers of attention and intelligent appreciation, the music of the eastern peoples of Europe has come very much into vogue. The Czech composers such as Smetana and Dvorak led the way, and the Slav composers followed by natural sequence. Even in the works of the Bohemian composers the proximity to the primitive temperamental man was much more apparent than in the much elaborated music of Teuton and Celtic races. And one of the tokens of the fact was this very practise of repeating little phrases over and over again, which has been so often observed to be the delight of the undeveloped savage."[121]

We are not surprised that the majority of composers did not find it necessary to study authentic Oriental music while scathing critics like Parry were ready to denounce them! Due to this negative aspect of Orientalism, music reflecting this branch of study was generally considered un-intellectual, and therefore was not placed in the same category as fugue, counterpoint, and the composition of a symphony.

Claude Debussy dared to consider Oriental music on a serious intellectual plane in contrast to many of his European colleagues. In 1887, the Minister of the Interior for the Dutch East Indies presented the Paris Conservatoire with a Javanese gamelan consisting of sixteen

---

[121] Ibid, source from handout.

instruments in *slendro*, the Javanese pentatonic scale. Debussy's use of the whole tone pentatonic scale is similar to the *slendro* gamelan tuning suggesting he was influenced by this set of instruments.[122] He also had the opportunity to view Javanese gamelans in the Paris Exhibitions of 1889 and 1890; apparently, this music left a lasting impression. Debussy was enthusiastic with Javanese music as he considered this eastern style presented many beneficial properties which could aid the progression of European music. He believed music had become stagnant due to Western composers' tendency to refer to musical masters of the past, i.e. Palestrina, Bach, Mozart, and Beethoven. Apparently he concluded music was failing to progress; one of his main ambitions was to free musical education from the confining, 'stuffy' academic rules placed upon it by the Germanic tradition:

"The worst of it is that the study of old works tends to lead the musician to manufacture, so to speak, copies from the antique, whereas each period must progress its own peculiar art, harmonizing with everything else. The age of aeroplanes has a right to its own music. Every musician should create the forms necessary to the expression of his genius. He should not employ standard forms, however admirable may have been the masters who established them in other days, with different motifs and without anticipating that they would become rigidly stereotyped.

---

[122] Sorrel, Guide to the Gamelan, p. 2.

Art must be spontaneous, music natural. What sometimes appears to be progress is in reality retrogression.

There have been, and, the evils of civilisation not withstanding, there still are, certain charming little races that learned music as naturally as one learns to breath. Their school of music is the eternal rhythm of the sea, the wind in the leaves and a thousand little noises that they eagerly listen to, without ever consulting standard text-books. Their only traditions are drawn from ancient songs mingled with dances, to which each one in his century added respectful contribution. The music of Java, however, is based on a counterpoint beside which that of Palestrina is child's play."[123]

It is intriguing to observe that Debussy places the contrapuntal aspect of Javanese music above Palestrina's work. In so doing, he made a gigantic statement by placing Oriental music on or above the same level as Western hierarchal tradition. Obviously, Debussy did not entertain the same opinions as Parry and other critics who derided the use of simple effects:

"And if setting aside European prejudice, we listen to the charm of their percussion instruments [referring to the Javanese gamelan], we are forced to

---

[123] Claude Debussy, source; Leon Vallas, translator Maire O'Brien, *The Theories of Claude Debussy — Musicien Français* (New York: Daver Publications, Inc., 1967), p. 17.

admit that in comparison ours produce but the barbaric noise of a travelling circus. The Annamites perform a kind of embryo lyric drama which they owe to Chinese influence, and in which the tetralogical formula may be discerned. Only there are more gods and less scenery. ... An excitable little clarinet directs emotion. A tom-tom provides the note of terror ... and that is all! There is no specially constructed theatre, no hidden orchestra. Only an instinctive need for art ingeniously satisfied; no trace of bad taste! And these people never thought of going to Munich in search of their formulas! What were they thinking of?" [124]

Debussy has defended the use of orchestral devises involving 'tone colouring' and musical simplicity as it satisfies artistic creation, and apparently displayed his impatience with prejudice fostered by Orientalism with his semi-sarcastic remarks. Accordingly, Debussy eagerly adopted Javanese techniques to progress Western music beyond this prejudicial, 'stale' environment that surrounded and suffocated him. While his music is not an absolute authentic representation of Javanese music, he introduced a new and invigorating form of Orientalism in music that was not necessarily used as a marketing ploy for the exotic music consumers. He ingeniously employed Javanese techniques as a method of progression and injected a fresh and revitalised approach to the

---

[124] Claude Debussy, ibid., pp. 22–23.

established 'antiquated' academic forms. In a letter to Pierre Louys dated 1895, Debussy wrote:

> "Do you not remember the Javanese music, able to express every shade of meaning, even unmentionable shades and which makes our tonic and dominant seem like ghosts?"[125]

A brief introduction to the basic principles of the gamelan and the construction of its music will enable us to understand and appreciate Debussy's adaptation of the musical qualities of the Javanese style. The gamelan is comprised of three sections, the phrase making instruments, the melodic instruments and the elaborating instruments; hence, music composed for the gamelan consists of layered textures. The phrase-making instruments are a series of bronze hanging gongs, and also bronze 'pot' gongs that sit inside a wooden frame on crossed chords. The *gong ageng* is the largest in the ensemble and considered the most sacred instrument of the gamelan. These instruments punctuate the melodic phrases, and may be compared to the bass section of a Western orchestra. The melodic 'middle' section of the gamelan contains *sarons*, small xylophone-type instruments with bronze plates, and *slentems*, instruments similar to the *sarons* but have thin brass plates suspended over bamboo resonators. These instruments play the melody of the composition, and may be similar to the string section of our orchestra, or the 'middle' voices of the tenor and alto sections in a choral composition. There are many instruments in the

---

[125] Sorrel, *Guide to the Gamelan*, p. 5.

elaborating section of the gamelan; the *bonangs* (pot gongs in a bed-type frame), the *kendang* (drums), the *gambang* (a wooden xylophone), the *gender* (smaller scaled *slentems*), the *rebab* (a two stringed bowed instrument), the *suling* (bamboo flute), the *celempung* and *siter* (zither instruments), and on occasions, singing may be introduced. This section may be considered similar to the woodwind and brass sections of the Western orchestra. As with Western orchestrations, the number of instruments varies depending on the composition performed and the availability of instruments in any particular gamelan.

The *bonangs* are the most important elaborating instruments generally found in all gamelans and are allocated three distinct styles (the *garap*) to elaborate the melody depending on the composition. We may trace these techniques in Debussy's adaptations; therefore, we will examine these elaborating procedures in more detail. The three techniques are called *gembyangan* (octaves), *mipil*, and *imbal*.

The *gembyangan* style is used when a composition features a melody with rests between each note; the *bonangs* play alternate interlocking patterns within the rests.

Figure I

Gembyangan Technique

The *mipil* technique features a repetition of melodic notes in compositions with a moderate or slow speed. The large *bonang* repeats two notes of the melody, and the smaller *bonang* plays the same two notes, but the tempo is doubled. Some notes may be omitted in order to avoid thickening the texture and creating dissonance.

Figure 2

Mipil Technique*

Melody	7		6		5		3

Lg. Bonang   7 6 7 . 7 6 7 6 5 3 5 . 5 3 5 3

Sm. Bonang   7 6 7 . 7 6 7 . 7 6 7 . 7 6 7 .   *etc.*

* Tones are indicated by numbers for Gamelan notation

The *imbal* technique is characterised by the interlocking of an on-beat pattern played by the large *bonang* with an off-beat pattern played by the smaller *bonang*. The two instruments sound notes with spaced intervals, thus when they perform together a fast ostinato is created which would be impossible for either *bonang* to accomplish if played separately.

Figure 3

Imbal Technique

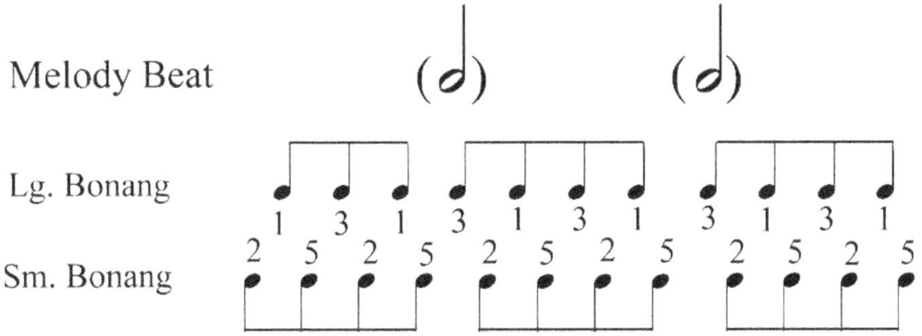

Melody Beat $\quad (\downarrow)$ $\quad (\downarrow)$

Lg. Bonang

```
1  3  1  3   1  3  1  3   1  3  1
2  5  2  5   2  5  2  5   2  5  2  5
```

Sm. Bonang

ostinato melody = 2 1 5 3 , etc.

Debussy's composition *Estampes* (1903) illustrates the assimilation of gamelan techniques in the first movement entitled *Pagodes.* In Bars 1–12, we may notice the layering of musical texture incorporating the vast range of the piano. The deep bass pedal notes resemble the sonorities and phrase punctuating aspect of the gongs; observe how Debussy phrased the music according to the bass notes. The melodic phrases in the soprano range are similar to the embellishing instruments of the gamelan, and the alto, tenor, and some sections of the baritone ranges represent the melodic aspect of the *sarons* and *slentems.* In addition, Debussy experiments with elaboration within certain sections such as Bars 12 and 62; the rhythmic patterns are reminiscent of the techniques encountered with the *bonangs.* For the construction of his melodies, he employed four distinct pentatonic scales illustrating the influence of the *slendro* tuning. Interestingly, Robert Schmitz has concluded Debussy structured this movement as an adaptation of Sonata form:[126]

❧ Exposition:

Bars 1–2; Introduction.

Bars 3–10; Subject I, introduced on the pentatonic black keys
of C#, D#, F#, G#, A#, and extends through the whole
movement in *ostinato*.

Bars 7–10; Subject II, in the tenor range, features the pentatonic mode
D#, C#, B, A#, G#.

Bars 11–14; Subject III (!), containing both elements of Subjects I and II
in   the mode of B, G#, F#, D#, C#.

Bars 15–18; Subject I returns.

❧ Development

Bars 19–22; Subject II developed.

Bars 23–26; Subject I developed.

Bars 27–30; Subjects I and II are combined, Subject I accompanies
Subject II in the left hand.

Bars 31–36; Subject IV (!), formulated from the second part of
Subject II in a different pentatonic mode, G#, B, C#, D#, E#.

Bars 37–44; Subjects I and II developed simultaneously.

Bars 45–53; Subject IV concluded the development section.

❧ Recapitulation

Bars 53–72; An exact recap. of bars 3–22.

Bars 73–77; A restatement of bars 11–14.

---

[126] Robert Schmitz, *The Piano Works of Claude Debussy* (U.S.A.: Duell, Sloan and Pearce Inc., 1950), pp. 83–84.

❧ Coda

Bar 38 onward.

It may be argued this movement is displayed as a typical product of Orientalism as the music supposedly depicts an oriental scene of pagodas in a 'dreamy' Western style reminiscent of the "Oriental Gaze." Yet, we observe Debussy was endeavouring to develop this concept of Orientalism to new heights; he has fused Western tradition, i.e. Sonata form, with his knowledge of the Javanese gamelan and its music, which other composers apparently had not previously attempted. Debussy did not resort to mere 'melodic flavouring' with Western orchestration to create an Oriental-sounding composition; he incorporated 'strange' pentatonic modes and unusual sonorities in contrast to 'academic' harmony, employing them as his subjects in sonata form, thereby formally including them with Western tradition rather than treating them as 'musical condiments'. Of course, one could argue these concepts are nothing more than an imitative experiment, an advanced method of creating authentic-sounding Oriental music for the 'exotic' market. It is my view that this is not so, Debussy adopted these techniques as his personal signature style in his creative musical compositions. He composed other works using these same techniques that were never intended to be considered a product of Orientalism.

As an example let us briefly examine his composition entitled *Masques* (1904); we note it has not received an Oriental title, therefore we may conclude this work was not intended to be orientalised, but rather display an infusion of this Eastern technique within his unique style of Western composition. We observe the

115

inclusion of 'strange' harmonies created by using intervals of a fifth and his amazing use of consecutive fifths in Bars 15–16, 19–21, indicating a complete departure from the traditional rules of Western harmony. This unusual treatment with the harmony may be influenced by his knowledge of the Javanese five-note *slendro* scale, and the textural structure may be considered similar to that of *Pagodes*. We can recognise the gong-style notes in the bass that punctuates the music into four-bar phrases, and in particular, the *bonang*-style rhythmic patterns similar to the *imbal* ostinato style. The contrapuntal layering texture typical of gamelan music may also be discerned at Bars 22–39. Therefore, it is obvious Debussy was developing and progressing his Western compositions by incorporating his knowledge of Oriental music.

We may also observe his 'Orientalism for Progress' technique in his composition *La Serenade Interrompu* as another example. Debussy adopts the 'exotic' in his use of a Moorish stylised melody to musically depict the serenading custom of Spain, using the techniques previously discussed; however, we must not consider this music primarily as an imitative work for the Oriental / exotic market. The prominent feature of this work is the *bonang* rhythmic *imbal* patterns running in semiquaver figures, and contrapuntal layers, i.e. those found at Bars 113–124.

Finally, we observe the most striking example of Debussy's 'Orientalism for Progress' in his composition *Les Tierces Alternees*, which as the title suggests, is structured exclusively on thirds. Noticeably this piece is based on the techniques adopted from the gamelan, and the contrapuntal textures have been included. We observe Debussy sectioned the music within three different staves;

this not only aids sight-reading as ledger notes may have been difficult to discern, but also visibly portrays the 'layered' aspect of the musical texture. We can also recognise his use of the gong-style bass notes in Bars 5–10, 14, 18, 32, 33, etc. This work is particularly astounding as it features an almost exact replica of the *bonang imbal* technique in its entire rhythmic structure. We may conclude this piece illustrates his triumphant accomplishment in his endeavour to 'break' the rules of Western harmony and tonality with his employment of thirds and the development of strange dissonances, creating new forms and techniques he had acquired through his knowledge of Orientalism. Contemporary composers such as Erik Satie admired Debussy for these achievements as he humorously noted in his comical *Conservatory Catechism* (1914):

CONSERVATORY CATECHISM

1. Dieubussy alone shalt thou adore
   And copy most perfectly.

2. Melodious never shalt thou be
   In deed nor in consent,

3. From plan shalt thou always abstain
   More easily to compose

4. With greatest care shalt thou violate
   The ancient rudimentary rules

5. Parallel fifths shalt thou create
   And octaves in like style

117

6. Never ever shalt thou resolve
   Dissonance of any kind

7. No piece shalt thou ever end
   With any consonant chord,

8. Ninths shalt thou accumulate
   Without the least discernment

9. Perfect harmony shalt thou not desire
   Except in marriage alone.

Ad gloriam tuam
ERIT SATIS
Amen.[127]

In conclusion, I hope I have successfully displayed to the reader Debussy's astounding and extraordinary adaptation of the techniques he acquired through his knowledge of Orientalism and exoticism in his music. We accept he was not attempting to compose authentic Oriental and foreign music; he was however displaying his originality. He did not endeavour to 'gaze at the East' in contrast to many other composers, but wished to learn from his experiences with Oriental tradition and culture, thus stripping away, in a sense, the prejudicial and racial veils that draped Orientalism. He did not attempt to assimilate Javanese music into Western accepted tradition; rather he turned the tables and pushed Western traditions to new

[127] Erik Satie. Source, Nigel Wilkins, ed. and trans., *The Writings of Erik Satie* (London: Ernst Eulenburg Ltd., 1980), p. 81. Wilkins' source; (S.I.M. 1914) S.I.M. = Société Internationale de Musique.

horizons through his knowledge of the gamelan. We observe he composed in a radical new dimension by breaking away from the old traditions of Western music with his adaptation of Javanese techniques. Through the years, the Javanese gamelan has become a particularly popular subject with the academic branch of Ethnomusicology; possibly Debussy's enthusiasm for the gamelan and its musical possibilities opened the doors for serious study and appreciation in contrast to the comical and primitive characterisations previously attributed to Eastern cultures. Undoubtedly Debussy made a tremendous contribution to Western art music through his unique Oriental techniques in music; we may conclude that his approach to Orientalism in music was most assuredly progressive and an inspirational legacy for the future.

❧◆❧

Andrew Lloyd Webber's *Phantom of the Opera*: An Example of the 'Musical Theatre Renaissance'

The modern day musical has become a particularly perplexing genre to contemplate and study. We are not presented with the popular post war variety dance 'skits' of the *Ziegfield Follies* which lacked a coherent dramatic plot, or 'musical plays' that incorporate musical numbers, e.g. *The King and I, Oklahoma, South Pacific, My Fair Lady*, etc., although these musicals are revived today. Ultimately, musical theatre became classified as a 'low-brow', popular entertainment for the masses in contrast to Classical opera. During the 1970s, and particularly the 1980s, musicals evolved into a new echelon — one might dare to call this era the "Musical Theatre Renaissance." Productions featured greater emphasis on the music with less importance placed on spoken dialogue similar to Classical opera tradition, and dance in general was gradually limited to apt sections of the plot if possible, i.e. if a scene is set at a ball, or if it was intended as a full musical dance production such as *CATS*. In addition, musicals also evolved as part of the popular culture scene, incorporating music styles such as rock and jazz, and cinematic influences regarding music and scenic production methods. Thus, a great divide exists concerning the exact nature of the modern day musical and where this form may be categorised culturally and academically. Are musicals modern day operas or a new genre for a new age? Are they a mere spectator entertainment, or do they have more to offer culturally?

I will attempt to address these various issues, selecting Lord Andrew Lloyd Webber's musical *The Phantom of the Opera* (1986) as an example of this evolutionary musical style. This choice will hardly surprise the reader, as Lloyd Webber is a giant within the musical theatre world; his works have been enjoyed and loved by millions despite the scathing criticisms hurled at his compositions. In 1982, he became the first composer to have three musicals running simultaneously in both New York and London; a truly amazing record he has continually repeated.[128] A concentration on just one of Lloyd Webber's works may not be considered the most appropriate procedure for studying the modern musical as it may be argued each musical is unique in its style, and one composition is not representative of the genre as a whole.   However, the same observation may be associated with the practise of collecting information through opinion polls; only a selection of the public are asked for their opinions, yet the polls aid in presenting a general view of the populace and are continually used as a research procedure.   We may consider the choice of *Phantom* as a selective representation; it contains many features now typical characteristics of the modern musical. In addition, this particular work was a major mile stone in Lloyd Webber's career as a composer; Michael Walsh points out that *Phantom* is the first musical where Lloyd Webber concentrated on key relationships within the score which illustrates a notable progressive leap from his earlier compositions.[129]   In

---

[128]   Programme note, *The Phantom of the Opera*, Theatreprint, Great Britain.
[129]   Michael Walsh, *Andrew Lloyd Webber; His Life and Works* (New York: Harry N. Adams Inc., 1997), p. 202.

October 1998, during an interview on the *Late Late Show* in Ireland, Lloyd Webber stated he loved all his musicals, but *Phantom* was particularly special to him. These factors contributed to the decision in selecting *Phantom* as a primary example of the modern day musical for this study.

When commencing the research for this essay I noticed many striking similarities with Wagnerian operatic culture concerning the categorisation of music of modernity, Lloyd Webber's *Phantom of the Opera*, the original story of the Phantom by Gaston Leroux, and the development of the modern musical. The German philosopher, Friedrich Nietzsche (1844–1900), declared that works of modernity displayed a polarisation of two extremes.[130] He concluded that Richard Wagner's operas were the best examples of the term 'modernity' owing to the two extremes of hystericism, (symbolised by effects, chromaticism, and feminisation of the drama and music), and asceticism (reflecting idealism, diatonic harmony, and religion in music), found within them. Nietzsche concludes works reflecting modernity are constructed with great contrasts and polarities that narrowly manage to remain stable within the composition to form a complete entity. I will refrain from stating that the modern musical contains 'sick' elements as Nietzsche harshly claimed was a feature of Wagner's music due to these polarities! However, we may observe similar contrasts concerning the Classical music / popular culture argument associated with the modern musical. Classical music may be interpreted as the ascetic, 'serious religious' element, while popular culture and the cinematic influences within musicals may be regarded the 'hysterical' element due to the implementation of

---

[130] Dr. Christopher Morris, Lectures, April 19, 1999.

special effects to capture mass appeal. In contrast to Nietzsche's opinion that polarities within works of modernity are in a state of repulsion, thus creating tension within the musical structure and the semblance of unity, I suggest the polarities within the modern musical are positive rather than negative factors as they pulsate a magnetic attraction and thus work in harmony while remaining recognisable as separate entities. These factors concerning the theory of modernity suggest that the modern musical has evolved from traditional classical opera to a new genre reflecting our contemporary era.

The German philosopher Theodor Adorno (1903–69) recognised that Wagner's operas were precursors of the film industry, hence we observe a connection between Classical 'high art' and 'low-brow' popular culture. Adorno wrote in his work *In Search of Wagner*:

> "Thus we see that the evolution of the opera, and in particular the autonomous sovereignty of the artists, is intertwined with the origins of the culture industry. Nietzsche, in his youthful enthusiasm, failed to recognise the artwork of the future in which we witness the birth of film out of the spirit of music."[131]

Adorno also considered that Wagner's use of the *leitmotiv* system, i.e. the organic development of music through musical motifs

---

[131] Theodor Adorno, *In Search of Wagner*, trans. Rodney Livingstone, (London: 1985), p.107, in David Huckvale, 'The Composing Machine; Wagner and Popular Culture', ed. Jeremy Tambling, *A Night at the Opera, Media Representations of Opera* (London, John Libbey and Co., Ltd., 1994), pp.116–117.

as a method to introduce a character's emotions or to represent a symbolic idea, had a particular connection with the function of film music:

> "The degeneration of the *leitmotiv* ... leads directly to cinema music where the sole function of the *leitmotiv* is to announce heroes or situations so as to help the audience orientate itself more easily."[132]

We should not overlook Wagner's various innovations at his theatre in Bayreuth that are reflective of film culture. He was the first composer to plunge the audience into darkness while an opera was performed, and his introduction of the hidden orchestra pit is similar in concept to the invisible soundtrack of a film. He also had a double proscenium constructed around the stage, distancing the audience representing reality and the 'real world' thus contrasting the illusory world of the opera. There were no side boxes in the auditorium, this design forced the audience to rivet its attention on the production, which is similar to the modern day silver screen of a cinema. Ultimately, Wagner may not only be regarded as an 'elite' opera composer in the Classical tradition, but also the 'father' of the popular culture industry; he is a 'bridge' spanning the polemic divide associated with works of modernity. Intriguingly, the productions of modern musicals, especially the *Phantom of the Opera*, have been influenced by the film industry; this subject will be examined later in more detail.

---

[132]   Ibid. *In Search of Wagner*, p. 46.

In this study, we will be examining the parallels between Wagner, Andrew Lloyd Webber and *Phantom of the Opera* as our example of the modern musical. It is hoped by using this method we may establish the theory of modernity as evidence that the modern musical of the middle to late twentieth century had entered a 'Renaissance Period' and evolved into a new genre separate from Classical opera.

Lord Andrew Lloyd Webber; a Composer of Modernity

Lord Andrew Lloyd Webber, [133] born on March 22, 1948, may be regarded as a true composer of modernity in that his musical training, experience, and interest encompasses both Classical tradition and popular music culture. Lloyd Webber commenced his musical studies at an early age; for his third birthday he received a gift of a violin, and later a French horn. He also attended piano lessons, but disliked learning the standard repertory of pieces that were required and preferred to compose his own works. Notwithstanding his preference for composing original music, Lloyd Webber was surrounded by Classical influences. His father, William ("Bill") Lloyd Webber, was an organ prodigy who gave concerts in London beginning at the age of ten. Lloyd Webber Sr. was gifted with the ability to recall and play a score upon hearing it, and could literally sight read any music placed before him, allowing him to obtain a secure professional career as a musician. He was one of the top students at the Royal College of Music, became the music director

---

[133] Walsh, *Andrew Lloyd Webber; His Life and Works*. The following information concerning Lloyd Webber's life has been based on this comprehensive source.

at two churches, a professor of composition and harmony at the Royal College of Music, and later was appointed director of the London College of Music. Lloyd Webber's mother, Jean, also received her musical education at the Royal College of Music and became a music teacher. His younger brother, Julian, is an astounding 'cellist who also studied the trumpet. Julian humorously described their musical household in his autobiography *Life with my 'Cello* (1986):

> "Life at Harrington Court … was chiefly memorable for the astonishing, ear-blowing volume of musical decibels which seemed to burst forth from every room most of the day and night. My father's electric organ, mother's piano, grandmother's deafening (she was deaf) television, elder brother's astounding piano and French horn, and my own scrapings on the 'cello and blowings on the trumpet themselves would have made the cannon and mortar effects of the *1812 Overture* seem a bit like the aural equivalent of a wet Sunday morning on the Hackney Marshes. …"[134]

Andrew Lloyd Webber's interests also extended to the realm of architecture and historical monuments, particularly those dating from the Victorian era. Interestingly, Lloyd Webber's first ambition career wise was to become chief inspector of ancient monuments in Britain. From the early age of ten, he wrote several sophisticated monographs on the subject, and at the age of thirteen sent a letter to

---

[134] Ibid. pp. 26–27.

the Ministry of Works lamenting the deplorable state and the lack of repair of various monuments.

During his youth, these early musical experiences and his love of architecture were gradually combined with his growing fascination with musical theatre. He became a regular 'theatre-buff' compliments of his Aunt Vi who brought him to see films such as *South Pacific* and *Gigi*, and also on cultural excursions to the West End where he became familiar with many hit musicals; the first live musical performance he attended was *My Fair Lady*. With his aunt's encouragement, he built a model theatre from bricks and boards, which included a gramophone turntable as a moveable stage in the round, similar to that found in the Palace Theatre in London. The little theatre also featured wings, flys, and a proscenium. With the help of his brother Julian, mini-productions were staged with toy soldiers, the 'orchestra' was a miniature military band; Julian moved all the figures while Andrew played the piano. His model theatre was no mere toy, but a valuable learning tool as Andrew staged several of the musicals he had seen, such as *Flower Drum Song* by Rodger and Hammerstein, as a unique method of studying their techniques and learning the basic principles associated with stage design. Andrew had also written his first composition for his model theatre entitled *The Toy Theatre*, from which excerpts were published in the magazine *Music Teacher* in 1959.

While attending Westminster Underschool for boys, Lloyd Webber was introduced to 'pop' music and listened regularly to Elvis, Bobby Vee, Bill Haely and the Comets, and the Everly Brothers. He also composed songs for several of the school shows; before the completion of his secondary education, he had already attracted attention as a budding composer and had signed on with the Noel Gay Organisation. (Gay had composed the music for *Me and My Girl*.) Later, Lloyd Webber recorded one of his school show songs called *Make Believe Love* with the assistance of a record producer named Charles Blackwell. Although this song was not released, he did not become discouraged and sent a demo tape to Decca Records, where upon making the usual rounds it was returned to Blackwell. This led to the publication of the song and the offer of an exclusive contract for Lloyd Webber with Southern Music. In addition, Blackwell was a client of Desmond Elliott, the publisher of Arlington Books, who showed an interest in Lloyd Webber's music. At this point, Lloyd Webber realised he required a talented lyricist for his music, and through his association with Elliott, he would be introduced to the lyricist he had been searching for, Tim Rice.

In the interim, Lloyd Webber had won a scholarship to attended Magdalen College at Oxford. He had been informed he would encounter several promising lyricists at Oxford, and therefore this encouraged his decision to accept the scholarship with the ulterior motive of scouting for talented lyricists. Before he moved to Oxford, Lloyd Webber had a meeting with Tim Rice, discovering their diverse preferences in music (Tim was a 'pop' fan who had never seen a musical, while Lloyd Webber preferred the music of the theatre). He suspected Rice was the lyricist he was searching for, however, he made no firm commitment immediately on this choice perchance he may discover a worthy lyricist at Oxford. During the first term, Lloyd Webber became disillusioned; he detested every minute of his sojourn in Oxford, and discovered it was not the 'Promised Land' overflowing with lyricists.

In 1965, Lloyd Webber decided to abandon Oxford in pursuit of his career as a professional musician with Rice. While many parents would have considered this a drastic choice and would be completely dismayed, Lloyd Webber's parents did not deter him from making this decision; this liberal attitude helped to advance his musical development. After leaving Oxford, Lloyd Webber enrolled in courses to further his musical education and develop his skills as a composer. He first attended a course in orchestration at the Guildhall School of Music, and later in 1967 studied orchestration at the Royal College of Music. Surprisingly, Lloyd Webber received unexpected advice from his father who believed he should not delay too long at the Royal Academy as their academic principles may undermine and destroy his own natural melodic gift. Lloyd Webber's father had a particular sensitivity concerning his son's musical education as Walsh observed:

> "This may tax the credulity of non-musicians, but Bill was right. In the mid-sixties, conservatories in both America and Europe were in the grip of twelve-tone fever, the academics having succumbed to the relentless proselytizing of the modernists. A young composer who wandered into their clutches writing like Dvorak would, a year later, wander out writing like Webern. Progressivism was the death of melody, deemed a hackneyed and useless relic of a discredited romantic past. Bill, an insider whose infatuation with romanticism was undiminished,

knew this perfectly well. By crippling Andrew's technique he very likely saved his soul."[135]

In the aforementioned *Late Late Show* interview, Lloyd Webber commented upon his father's logic concerning his advice to leave the Royal College of Music, stating his father did not want the popular style of music he had 'absorbed' and which came naturally to be 'taught out of him' as it was the musical language of his generation. As we may observe, Lloyd Webber's musical development originated from the Classical 'high art' idealism in combination with his knowledge and experience with popular music culture which was not discredited during his youth as a 'low-brow' style.

Within his compositions, we notice his inclusion of both sides of the cultural spectrum. The popular elements, i.e. rock, jazz, and cinematic influences with special effects are obvious, while many Classical music influences are also discerned. Lloyd Webber acquired an interest in contemporary Russian music through his father; Prokofiev's style can be heard in *Jesus Christ Superstar* in the song "Pilate and Christ" with his use of G-minor and F sharp- minor chords.[136] During the crucifixion scene, there are also influences of Ligeti present.[137] For the New York production of *CATS*, the scene featuring Growltiger was included with music reminiscent of *Madame Butterfly* composed by Puccini. In *Phantom of the Opera*, the Classical influences are particularly obvious as the work is set within the Paris Opéra; there are references to the grand operas of

---

[135] Ibid. pp. 36–37.
[136] Ibid. p. 69.
[137] Ibid. p.71.

Meyerbeer, parodies of classical operas composed by Salieri, and the futuristic developments of Debussy and Wagner are evident which will be discussed later.

Of noticeable interest, many musical composers were also influenced by the polemical principles of Classical and popular culture in their training and experience. Gershwin, already well established on Broadway, later received formal training in counterpoint and harmony; also, Cole Porter studied music with Vincent d'Indy in Paris.[138] Joseph Swain also observed that similar examples of Classical influences with composers of musical theatre are more apparent within the later half of the twentieth century. For instance, Stephen Sondheim, a musical theatre contemporary with Lloyd Webber, studied composition with Milton Babbitt.[139] In addition, we observe the influence of Puccini's opera *Madame Butterfly* within the works of Alain Boublil and Claude-Michel Schoenberg as with *Miss Saigon*, and the song "Bring Him Home" from *Les Miserables* with a theme similar to the famous "Humming Chorus". In summary, we may argue composers of modern day musicals bridge the divide between Classical and popular culture; assuredly, we may consider Lloyd Webber a true composer of modernity.

The Phantom of the Opera and the Wagnerian Connections

---

[138] Joseph P. Swain, *The Broadway Musical, A Critical and Musical Survey* (Oxford University Press, 1990), p. 9.
[139] Ibid.

Contrary to popular conceptions, Lloyd Webber was not the first composer to attempt the task of setting the classic tale of the Phantom as a musical. In the United States several attempts to stage Gaston Leroux's story occurred, and in East London, Ken Hill directed a comic version in 1984 with liberal musical borrowings from classical opera composers, including Mozart, Gounod, Verdi, Offenbach and Donizetti. Lloyd Webber read a review of the latter version in the London *Daily Mail* and contacted Cameron Mackintosh for his opinion. Mackintosh considered the subject had possibilities and arranged a screening of the 1925 classic silent film featuring Lon Chaney as the Phantom. According to George Perry, Lloyd Webber and Mackintosh were impressed and described the film as 'evocative'.[140] Subsequently they viewed the 1943 film remake with Claude Rains, the next Hollywood actor to don the mask; however, Mackintosh relates they had not discovered the magnetic "Eureka" quality they were still seeking.[141] Not long after they attended a production of Ken Hill's version and considered reproducing it featuring an extended range of operatic material with the notion of commissioning Hill to revise the material. Lloyd Webber admits they had "something like *The Rocky Horror Show* in mind."[142] They sought the advice of Jim Sharman, director of *The Rocky Horror Show*, and endeavoured to capture his interest in their idea of a musical with a chase scene in the cellars of the Paris Opéra resembling an Indiana Jones action packed adventure.[143] Sharman

---

[140] George Perry, *The Complete Phantom of the Opera* (New York: Henry Holt and Company Inc., 1988), p. 66.
[141] Cameron Mackintosh, 'The Phantom's Trail', *Phantom Souvenir Programme* (London: Dewynters Plc., 1986, 1994)
[142] Perry, ibid.
[143] Ibid.

was of the opinion Hill's version was far too comical and suggested that unless Lloyd Webber composed the score, the musical would not be interesting. Lloyd Webber and Mackintosh both agreed and decided to drop the project.

Fate, however, was to intervene nine months later when Lloyd Webber happened across a copy of the original novel published in 1911 by Gaston Leroux in a second hand bookshop in New York. Mackintosh discovered a copy concealed in a collection of books belonging to his aunt. Upon reading the original novel, Lloyd Webber's perception of the tragic tale was favourably altered and he decided a serious treatment of the subject was preferable. He later explained that with *Phantom* he discovered what he was always looking for — a romantic plot:

> "I was actually writing something else at the time, one of the earliest treatments of my 1989 musical, David Garnett's *Aspects of Love*, and I realised that the reason why I was hung up was because what I was trying to write was a major romantic story, and I had been trying to do that ever since I started my career, but I had never been able to find the plot that could be my — er — as it were — *South Pacific*. Then, with *Phantom*, it was there! I called Cameron and said, "I think if I follow the romance in the novel it could be the plot I'm looking for — I'll give it a go." "[144]

---

[144] Ibid. pp. 67–68.

He was particularly impressed with the character of Christine in the novel for she promises to return to the Phantom before his death and return the ring she had received from him. Could it be possible that Lloyd Webber realised he was attracted to one of the apparent Wagnerian links in the novel that are an integral part of the story?

The Novel: a Product of Wagnerism?

The first important Wagner connection within Leroux's novel is the concept of a rejected man, an outcast like the Phantom, may be redeemed through the self-sacrifice and love of a woman as we observe in the case of Goethe's classic drama *Faust*. Throughout the novel by Leroux there are specific references to Gounod's opera *Faust* based on Goethe's drama; interestingly Wagner was also influenced by Goethe's classic which is evident in his compositions such as *A Faust Overture* and the *Flying Dutchman*. Additionally, the Phantom sardonically compares himself to Don Juan through his composition *Don Juan Triumphant,* (in contrast to the cavalier who is the epitome of romanticism to women, he is an object of derision due to his deformity); incidentally, Don Juan was affiliated with the anti-hero Faust in the Romantic Era.

Of particular interest is the portrayal of how the Phantom, Erik, is redeemed. Approaching the conclusion of the novel, Erik threatens that unless Christine marries him, they would all meet their demise with his destruction of the opera house by igniting his own private arsenal of gunpowder hidden in the cellars. She agrees to his demand, whereupon Erik floods the room containing the deadly ammunition by diverting water from the underground lake. However, Raoul, Christine's fiancé, and a character simply referred to as the Persian, attempt to rescue Christine from Erik's lair, but are trapped in the gunpowder storeroom and are at the point of drowning. Christine pleads with Erik to save their lives, and promises to be his "living wife" rather than a reluctant wife held as a prisoner. When Erik has freed Raoul and the Persian, returning them to ground level, Christine kisses him for the first time and he is struck by a 'cosmic knowledge' similar to Wagner's Parsifal who receives a kiss from Kundry and realises that compassion is the answer to heal Amfortas' wound. Erik through his newfound compassion realises that he cannot hold Christine to her promise and frees her for she loves another. Erik is also comparable to the character of Amfortas in that he bears a wound, his disfigurement, which has caused him to be isolated as an object of public scorn. Through Christine's kiss, he is healed and his only remaining wish is to die, stating that he has tasted all the happiness the world can offer. In this instance, Erik also resembles the god Wotan from the *Ring Cycle* in that he only wishes for the end. Wagner once wrote of his character Wotan, "he rises to the tragic height of willing his own destruction. This is the lesson that we have to learn from human history; to will the inevitable and carry it out ourselves."[145] While Wagner's statement is controversial in the extreme, we note his character Wotan wishes to take the inevitable into his own hands, thus creating the illusion he had the freedom to do so, therefore making the inevitable bearable.

---

[145] Wagner, letter to August Röckel, 25 January 1854.

The second important Wagnerian connection within Leroux's novel is the contrast between the acquisition of power and the quest for love symbolised by a simple gold ring. The philosopher Claude Levi-Strauss (b. 1908) observed that in Wagner's *Ring Cycle* there must be an exchange between the two emotions; we must choose one or the other, as it is impossible to obtain both simultaneously. The god Wotan desires possession of the magic ring forged from the stolen gold belonging to the Rhine Maidens, yet does not wish to relinquish love which is the price to possess it. Erik as the Phantom is a god-like figure, freely wielding his power and control over the opera house. He has astounding capabilities as a gifted musician, architect, inventor, and is a master in the realm of illusion and magic. He also possesses a magnificent tenor voice with the capability to hypnotise. Regardless of all these attributes, he is devoid of the basic happiness that the ordinary man may aspire to; Erik wishes to have a loving wife and live a reasonably normal life above ground. Unlike Wotan, Erik recognises the exchange required for the possession of love and is prepared to relinquish all of his power at the opera house for this ideal. Yet, he commandeers love as a token of power through his present of the wedding ring to Christine, and therefore the exchange has not been properly executed. When Erik first conducts Christine to his home on the lake, she displays a false sense of courage to obtain his trust whereby she may regain her liberty. She succeeds in persuading him to release her; extracting a promise from her to return, Erik gives her the gold ring. Christine explains its significance to Raoul in the novel:

(Raoul) "Oh, so Erik gave you that ring!"

(Christine) "You know he did, Raoul! But what you don't know is that, when he gave it to me, he said, 'I give you back your liberty, Christine, on condition that this ring is always on your finger. As long as you keep it, you will be protected against all danger and Erik will remain your friend. But woe to you if you ever part with it, for Erik will have his revenge!'"[146]

In this instance, Erik is similar to Siegmund from *Die Walkure* of the *Ring Cycle* who upon taking the sword from the tree proclaimed this action was executed for the sake of love; Siegmund had acquired an object of power for the wrong reason. Apparently, the fate of those who do not complete the exchange between love and power is grim. Brunhilde, the daughter of Wotan, returns the magic ring to the Rhine where it belongs thus causing the demise of the gods of Valhalla. This is similar to the conclusion of Leroux's novel; when Erik's death approaches, he sends for Christine who keeps her promise and returns the ring to him. Erik ultimately loses Christine and wishes for the end. Slivoj Zizek developed Levi-Strauss' theory of the symbolic love and power exchange by proposing that apart from the precondition of sacrificing love or power, there must also be a balance as the emotion we desire has to be controlled.[147] We cannot wield unlimited power as with Alberich from the *Ring Cycle* who forges the magic ring, eventually he becomes a powerless dwarf, nor can we experience unrestrained love as with Siegmund who shatters ethical conventions and marries his sister, the punishment

---

[146] Gaston Leroux, *The Phantom of the Opera* (United States: Dorset Press, 1988), p. 147.
[147] Dr. Morris, Lectures, February 22, 1999.

for their crime was death. Leroux apparently had discovered one further restriction; even if the power and love exchange is complete, the love one experiences cannot be sustained unless the person who is loved returns the same feelings. In addition, the person who is the object of your affections cannot be forced to love you, a risk must be taken when relinquishing power; hopefully the feeling of love will be reciprocated. In summary, love must be returned if the exchange is to succeed.

In Leroux's novel, we may also detect references to the cultural influences effected by Wagner's music and ideology apart from the direct symbolic and philosophical links with his operas. With the emergence of the Wagnerian movement later in the nineteenth century, a progression towards a new austere social code occurred; the contemporary ideology advocated the separation of music from all social activities considered frivolous.[148] Ironically, Meyerbeer's grand operas with their inclusion of grandiose scenic effects pandering to mass appeal were deemed inappropriate and incongruous with the elitist conceptions associated with music. Leroux includes an anti-Meyerbeer reference in his novel; apparently, the Phantom is supportive of these contemporary aesthetics:

> "Mademoiselle, to celebrate our wedding, you
> shall make a very handsome present to a few hundred
> Parisians who are at this moment applauding a poor

---

[148] William Webber, *Wagner, Wagnerism, and Musical Idealism*, p. 29, from a lecture handout, Dr. Morris, 1999.

masterpiece of Meyerbeer's: you shall make them a present of their lives."[149]

Concerning the musical aesthetics of that period, Bryan Mage explains Wagner was interested in portraying human emotion through his music dramas:

> "[Wagner's] music drama ... would be about the insides of characters. It would be concerned with their emotions, not their motives. It would explore and articulate the ultimate reality of experience, what goes on in the heart and soul. ... What Wagner thought he had done above all else was develop an art-form that made possible the expression, and hence the experience, of unbounded feeling about specific things — what he called 'emotionalizing of the intellect'."[150]

Leroux strengthens the Wagnerian connection with the Phantom's character through Christine's description of Erik's masterpiece, *Don Juan Triumphant:*

> "Presently, I began to understand Erik's contemptuous phrase when he spoke about operatic music. What I heard now was utterly different from what had charmed me up to then. His *Don Juan Triumphant* ... seemed to me at first one awful, long,

---

[149] Leroux, *Phantom*, p. 242.
[150] Bryan Mage, *Aspects of Wagner* (Oxford University Press: 1988), pp. 8–9.

magnificent sob. But little by little, it expressed every emotion, every suffering which mankind is capable. It intoxicated me. …."[151]

Undoubtedly, Leroux was advocating Wagner's concept of 'emotionalising the intellect' through music.

Simultaneously, within the novel there is an underlying religious connection corresponding with salvation theology that is reminiscent of Wagner's *Parisfal.* This connection is not obvious on first inspection for two reasons. First, the novel intimates Catholic associations and symbols which would have been apparent to contemporary readers, but owing to the reformations and development of the modern Church, have become obscured through the passage of time. Second, Leroux was an admirer of Edgar Allen Poe and his writings were influenced by his style of gothic horror; therefore, elements mistaken as strange and bizarre eccentricities may actually have a deep religious significance. One of these elements is portrayed particularly with Erik's unusual décor, when he introduces Christine to his underground lair she is startled by the ominous surroundings:

" 'This is my room, if you care to see it, it is rather curious.' His manners, his words, his attitude gave me confidence and I went in without hesitation. I felt as if I were entering a mortuary chamber. The walls were all hung with black but, instead of the white tears that usually relieve that funeral

---
[151]   Leroux, *Phantom*, p. 142.

upholstery, there was an enormous stave of music with the notes of the *Dies Irae*, many times repeated. In the middle of the room was a canopy, from which hung curtains of red brocaded stuff, and, under the canopy, an open coffin. 'That is where I sleep,' said Erik. 'One has to get used to everything in life, even eternity.'."[152]

The cryptic meaning of this passage may be clarified by another section in the novel, if we can interpret the veiled clues; Erik abducts Christine a second time during a performance of *Faust* while she is singing the role of Marguerite. While in his lair she passes the time reading a Catholic devotional book entitled the *Imitation of Christ*; we must assume this book belongs to Erik, certainly she did not carry it during her performance, and it is unlikely he would allow her to return to her dressing room to retrieve any personal items. In addition, if she did regain her freedom, it is probable she would not return to his lair as she was planning to elope with Raoul that night. Therefore, we can assume Erik contemplated the contents of this book containing a chapter concerning the practise of meditating on death for the good of the soul:

"Very quickly will there be an end of thee here; take heed there-fore how it will be with thee in another world. To-day man is, and tomorrow he will be seen no more. And being removed out of sight, quickly also is out of mind. ... Thou oughtest in every

---

[152] Ibid. p.139.

deed and thought so to order thyself, as if thou wert to die this day. If thou hadst a good conscience thou wouldst not greatly fear death. ... Happy is the man who hath the hour of his death always before his eyes, and daily prepareth himself to die. If thou hast ever see one die, consider that thou also shalt pass away by the same road."[153]

This chapter apparently left a striking impression upon Erik as his surroundings are constant reminders of mortality. Apart from having witnessed many deaths, he has caused many deaths by his own hand while securing the secrecy of his lair; in preparing for his own death in this extreme manner, we realise how deeply he is tormented by his conscience. This may explain the display of the *Dies Irae* on the walls as it is foremost a prayer begging God for mercy. In addition, he insists on performing his victims' Requiem; evidently, he is consumed with guilt for the murders he has committed and is particularly concerned with the welfare of their souls despite the Persian's description of the Phantom as an amoral character. The question of redemption is particularly important in the novel.

Considering these Wagnerian influences, it would be intriguing to discover if Leroux was a Wagnerian supporter. He had a particular interest in the theatre before he commenced his study of law, which may have remained an important factor in his life; when he abandoned his career as a lawyer, his first assignments as a journalist for a newspaper were in drama criticism and courtroom

---

[153] Thomas A. Kempis, *The Imitation of Christ, Book I Chapter XXII*, ed. Charles Eliot, *The Harvard Classics* (New York: P.F. Collier and Son Corp., 1963), p. 230.

reporting. His novel may have been a product of a possible interest in Wagnerian philosophy and literature.

Lloyd Webber's Production

Within Lloyd Webber's musical, several of these important Wagnerian elements are retained, including the ring, and the Phantom's redemption symbolically bestowed by Christine's kiss. In addition, Levi-Strauss' theory concerning the exchange between power and love is dramatically visible as the plot progresses and the characters within the opera house realise the Phantom is a mortal man. Initially he is believed to be a ghost, and therefore is considered a god-like figure, safe from detection, exercising considerable power over the Opéra staff by manipulating their fears and superstitions. In the progression of the musical, the characters gradually discover he is a mortal man though he continues to be a considerable entity to be reckoned with; this is apparent in the Masquerade scene when he materialises as Red Death and dramatically delivers his score of *Don Juan Triumphant*, demanding that the management produce his opera. Finally, he secretly assumes the leading tenor's role in the production of *Don Juan* and uses this opportunity to propose to Christine; here he is publicly declaring his desire to live a normal life, the omnipresent and formidable Phantom has surrendered his power for the love of Christine. Now that his secret is revealed, his defences have been stripped away, allowing the opera house staff to pursue him in the caverns that were once his safe haven. This development is not derived from the original novel as the Phantom's nature and identity remains undisclosed to everyone, with the exception of Christine, Raoul, and the Persian; it is fascinating to witness this gradual exchange within the musical. Apparently, this development was influenced by the various film remakes, particularly the 1925 version where the avenging mob eventually kill Erik.

On further inspection, there is evidence of a Wagnerian link corresponding to Zizeck's philosophy of limitations regarding the symbolic exchange of love and power. The Phantom's love for Christine within the musical is presented as a passionate and physical attraction in a particular manner implying their relationship is illicit in nature similar to Siegmund and Sieglinde of Wagner's *Ring Cycle*. Lloyd Webber retained the original concept of the Phantom's composition, *Don Juan Triumphant*, and adapted the idea for a particular purpose; in the musical, the Phantom has composed this work as an opera for Christine containing lyrics of a passionate nature. As mentioned earlier, the Phantom secretly assumes the leading role and takes 'Freudian' pleasure in the fact Christine sings the intense lyrics to him unaware of his presence. Hal Prince, the director, and Maria Björnson, the production designer, wished to reflect that a deformed person had the right to a normal love life in all respects. However, we may conclude as the Phantom has deceived Christine in this particular manner the producers' initial concept is lost and therefore we may detect an unsavoury element, as the Phantom is no longer portrayed as the restrained, dignified gentleman of the novel. This illicit association is also reflected in the scenery design as Björnson explained in an interview for the Cameron Mackintosh and Really Useful Group 'Phantom' Website:

> Q. In a general sense, the sculptures around the proscenium arch help to convey a particular mood to the entire work, but in what way do they specifically relate to the story? How do they symbolize the relationships between the main characters?

> R. Hal Prince and I had long discussions about people who were deformed fell in love. This was their right as well. We decided to choose nymphs and satyrs to show the feelings of lust between opposites in a Victorian theatrical way. Trying to attain the impossible.[154]

Lust?! Whatever happened to pure romantic love? Therefore, in Lloyd Webber's production, the concept of limitations is evident; love cannot be without its restraints and certain restrictions. In addition, the character of Christine in this production is not the complete innocent portrayed in the novel, as she slightly resembles Kundry in Wagner's *Parsifal*. Kundry has a dual personality; she sways from the seducer to an image of Mary Magdalen the penitent. In her role as seducer, which remains ambiguous, she inflicts a

---

[154] 'The Musical, Illusion — Backstage Interviews', *The Phantom of the Opera, United States,* Website: Cameron Mackintosh and the Really Useful Group — http://www.thephantomoftheopera.com/musical/illusion/backstage.html

symbolic wound upon Amfortas who becomes an outcast among his fellow Knights of the Grail. Christine in the musical reveals the Phantom's wound before the public, i.e. his disfigurement, as she strips his mask away during *Don Juan Triumphant* when she realises he has assumed the leading role. In addition, Leroux's implied theory that love must be reciprocated and never forced is apparent; their relationship within the musical is doomed to failure.

A religious connotation may be recognised within the musical that strengthens the similarities with Wagner's *Parsifal*. In the famous scene where the Phantom leads Christine to his home on the lake, hundreds of candles mysteriously rise out of the depths. Björnson explained she wished their journey to assume a ritualistic ambience we associate with a church environment.[155] Strikingly this is reminiscent of Parisifal's mystic journey to Montserrat with the knight Gurnemanz who explains time becomes space as one travels to the sacred Castle of the Grail. Additionally, Björnson commented this scene was intended to represent repressed sexuality,[156] and this is a particular issue within *Parsifal*.

Wagnerian links within the production methods of this musical are also apparent. As previously mentioned, there is an obvious tendency to restrict dance to appropriate sections of the drama. Wagner disapproved of the inclusion of dance within opera, diminishing its role within the drama to mere gestures enacted by the performers. Apparently, Wagner's attitude towards dance was affected by the frivolous nature of his audiences and their expectations regarding this spectacle, Lloyd Webber commented

---

[155] Website; ibid.
[156] Ibid.

upon the Parisian mentality for ballet that disrupted a production of Wagner's *Tannhauser*:

> "Key also to the Paris formula was the ballet. This was usually at the start of Act III. The gentlemen could dine before arriving at the theatre in time to see their various young ladies in the corps de ballet. Wagner's *Tannhauser* caused an uproar with the Jockey Club because its ballet was placed too early in the production for their members' convenience."[157]

Within the production of *Phantom*, ballet has been restricted to the grand opera sequences where it would traditionally be featured, and to sections showing the working life of the Paris opera house where the *corps de ballet* was essential. The choreographer Gillian Lynne studied contemporary dance styles in an effort to portray historical accuracy.[158] In addition, the *corps de ballet* are important characters within the initial chapters of the original novel as they introduce and set the backdrop by their accounts of the mysterious legend of the Phantom, and therefore the dancers have an important role within the drama. Dance has also been restricted to appropriate sections of the plot as with the Masquerade scene where dancing contributes to the integrity of the musical. Moreover, the gestures of the characters are important and are indicated in the piano rehearsal scores similar to Wagner who slavishly marked the actions for his characters. In one instance, Buquet, the chief of the

---

[157] Andrew Lloyd Webber, 'The Paris Opera House', *Phantom Souvenir Programme* (London: Dewynters Plc., 1986, 1994).
[158] Perry, *Complete Phantom*, p. 72.

flies, is requested to explain why a backdrop came crashing down during a rehearsal; when he replies "… it must be a ghost," the score indicates he is to 'smirk unpleasantly'. Also, Meg, a member of the *corp de ballet* is directed to look up as she sings, "He's here, the Phantom of the Opera … ." Additionally, the placing of cast members in certain areas of the stage as the plot progresses was deemed important, especially where the Phantom was concerned. His stage movements and actions were carefully worked out according to the design of his mask as Björnson relates:

> "When we discussed the Phantom's costume, I was concerned that he would be stuck behind a mask all evening. My assistant reminded me of a half-mask I wore to a fancy dress costume ball given by Sarah Brightman and Andrew Lloyd Webber. This enabled the actor to have a facial contact with his audience. … When we first put the show on, there was a lot of discussion with Michael Crawford [as to] which side of the face the mask should be [on]. A week later he requested to change the side. He had worked out all the moves. He was absolutely right! This way in the first lair scene he mainly moves from the organ to the lair mirror where Christine is, showing his good side. In the second lair scene he is facing the opposite side of the stage. The mask is off and we see the 'bad side' of his face."[159]

---

[159]   Website; ibid.

In the piano rehearsal scores, for obvious practical reasons, the dialogue sections and the actions that are intended to occur as the musical progresses are inserted between the sections of music, in a similar fashion to a Wagner score.

The next obvious Wagner parallel concerns the decision reached by the producers to leave certain 'blanks' within the storyline of *Phantom*. Wagner disliked the practise of including too many dramatic details within opera, as he believed this led to the entanglement of the plot within social and political issues.[160] He preferred to concentrate on the emotions of the characters; therefore, this would require the stripping of the plot of superfluous details down to the bare bones. Within *Phantom*, character interaction is paramount, yet amazingly many details of the plot purposely remain 'blank' according to Hal Prince as he stated they wanted the audience to use their imagination and therefore decided to omit various sections. The following is a list of the details purposely edited:

    ❧   The Phantom's early life, the circumstances leading to his tenure at the opera house, and the first time he espies Christine.

    ❧   The Phantom's existence when Christine leaves him, and what becomes of him in the last moment of the musical.

    ❧   The possibility of Christine meeting the Phantom again.

    ❧   Christine and Raoul's first meeting.

    ❧   Christine's relationship with her father, a famous violinist in Sweden.

    ❧   The Phantom's first encounter with Madame Giry.

---

[160]   Mage, Aspects of Wagner, pp. 7–8.

❧ The friendship between Christine and Meg Giry, and how their relationship progresses.

❧ Christine and Raoul's life after their experience with the Phantom, and how this experience had affected their lives.[161]

Notably, these 'blanks' within the plot afford a convenient opportunity for the production of a sequel, and this may have been intended. In 1999, Frederick Forsyth wrote a continuation of the Leroux classic entitled *The Phantom of Manhattan* that was suggested by Lloyd Webber who had seriously considered composing a sequel to his original musical. However, Forsyth maintained Leroux's writing and plot construction was of inferior quality, claiming Lloyd Webber's musical was the only logical version thereby justifying the complete makeover of the original Phantom legend to facilitate his expediency in filling the 'blanks' mentioned above.[162] However, due to the sweeping changes within this new version, it received adverse reactions and the project to compose the sequel was postponed indefinitely as far as we are aware.

Hypothetically, a link to Wagner's *Ring Cycle* exists with the possibility of creating a prequel rather than a sequel. Originally, Wagner composed an opera featuring Siegfried, discovering that the character's background was not developed fully to his satisfaction; subsequently, he decided to compose a prequel to establish the background in more detail. However, still not satisfied with the result, Wagner composed prequel after prequel until the *Ring Cycle*

[161] Website, ibid. 'Study guide, Filling in the Blanks' — http://www.thephantomoftheoprera.com/history/studyguide/blanks.html

[162] Frederick Forsyth, *The Phantom of Manhattan* (Great Britain: Bantam Press, 1999), pp. 5–27.

was completed. *Phantom of the Opera* fans in general have expressed their preference for a prequel, in contrast to Forsyth's proposed continued edition, as they do not agree with his changes to the original classic. The new version suggested by fans for consideration is Susan Kay's novel *Phantom*.[163] Kay, influenced by Lloyd Webber's musical, was impressed with the fact the concept of the Phantom's redemption had been retained. She wished to present a story that developed the background of the mysterious Phantom that was left ambiguous in Leroux's novel with the exception of a brief outline in the epilogue. Of notable interest, Kay develops the concept of the symbolic exchange of love for power. Erik accepts the fact, due to his deformity, he will possibly never receive unconditional love as he learned from experience by his mother's rejection, and acknowledges the acquisition of power as a preferable substitute. In addition, Kay addresses Erik's spirituality, and aptly portrays his respect for nature and its universal innocence that parallels Wagner's philosophy concerning the 'sacred' value of nature and living creatures exemplified in *Parsifal*. Accordingly, if Lloyd Webber, at some future date considered adapting Kay's version, the Wagnerian links would be perpetuated.

Due to the philosophical and aesthetical connections with Wagnerism, the above-mentioned issues concerning Lloyd Webber's *Phantom* may be considered parallel to Classical 'high-art' idealism. To compliment and complete the comparison with the theory of modernity, we will now present the similarities with the production of *Phantom*, and the elements of Wagnerism perceived as the precursors of popular mass culture, namely the film industry.

---

[163] Susan Kay, *Phantom* (New York: Island Books, Dell Publishing, Delacorte Press, 1991, 1993).

Wagner's innovations regarding stage effects may be described as 'proto-Hollywood'. At the conclusion of *Rhinegold* of the *Ring Cycle*, Wotan and the gods enter the celestial palace of Valhalla by walking over a rainbow. In *Parsifal*, a magnificent scrolling backdrop was employed as Gurnemanz escorts Parsifal to Monserrat, thus the effect of time becoming space was simulated, giving the impression they had walked miles when in reality they moved only a few paces. This unique effect astounded contemporary audiences who were not accustomed to moving pictures in contrast to the public of this modern age familiar with television and cinematic productions.

Notably, the various film interpretations of the Phantom legend played an important role in Lloyd Webber's production regarding its scenic construction. Björnson, influenced by the scenery of the 1925 film, desired to recapture that seamless, flowing action in the descent through the cellars:

"I liked the fact that one scene flowed into another. I tried to keep it as 'light' and 'filmic' as possible. ... I was struck by how close he was [the set designer] to the original Paris Opera house and how much he makes of the first journey down to the lake. I felt it did two things; a) build up great expectations for what was to come, and b) go into our subconscious rather like a dream. This really interested me, so I attempted to do it on stage. I like the idea that everything would slowly get more and more secret."[164]

In an endeavour to maintain the 'flowing' ambience of the scene on stage, two sets of doubles perform the Phantom and Christine's descent to the lair on moveable ramps thus intensifying the effect.[165]

Special effects, which we may also attribute to cinematic presentations, comprise the falling chandelier and the Phantom descending with the angel sculpture during the Roof scene. In addition, Paul Daniels, a specialist with illusions, was commissioned to develop the magic effects that include the Phantom's ability to disappear and reappear, shoot fireballs from a staff, and then vanish at the conclusion of the show directly in view of the audience.[166] Critics may argue these elements are designed for mere spectacle, however, we must not overlook the fact the Phantom was a master magician and therefore these effects are integral to the drama.

Notwithstanding these sensational effects, the production designers desired that the musical would essentially be a product of, by, and for the theatre. Hal Prince stated:

> "It's not a simple show but it's not an enormous technological show. We took advantage of the working Victorian Machinery — we could have it staged it in the same way had we opened when the

---

[164] Website; ibid. 'Illusion –Backstage' —
http://www.thephantomoftheopera.com/musical/illusion/backstage.html

[165] Perry, *Complete Phantom*, pp. 80–81.
[166] Ibid. p. 72.

theatre was first built. In New York we shall adapt
the Majestic Theatre in a similar way."[167]

Björnson also wished to develop scenic effects that would be
singularly successful on the stage; it is her opinion that if the stage
production was captured on film, the same effect would not be
successfully conveyed.[168] Ironically, the cinema has returned to its
genesis — the theatre! This brings to mind the fact that astonishing
an audience with spectacular scene changes accomplished in full
view is not a new concept; it was common practise in Italian *opera
seria* in Baroque times as with Handel's operas in London during the
1700s.

Controversial to our perceptions regarding a live
performance, *Phantom* contains several pre-recorded sequences
reminiscent of Wagner's hidden orchestra pit as the precursor to
cinematic soundtracks mentioned previously. These sections are
used for the purpose of practicality, as with the descent to the lair
scene where the doubles must lip-synchronise to maintain the
fluidity of the action, and with scenes where the performers are
preparing for the next scene changes while their characters need to
be heard off or onstage. *The Phantom Appreciation Website*[169] lists
the sequences that are pre-recorded, although depending on each
production, several of these sections may be performed live:

---

[167]   Ibid. p. 74.
[168]   Website, ibid.
[169]   *The Phantom Appreciation Website*: 'Secrets of the Show' —
http://phantom.simplenet.com/record.htm

Pre-recorded Scenes

- The Overture
- The Phantom's lines of the "Notes Scene" in the manager's office
- The Phantom's laughter as he murders Buquet, and drops the chandelier
- Red Death's lines as he descends the staircase, the rest of the cast is live
- When the Phantom mocks the police as they secure the opera house in their attempt to capture him
- The manager's lines as they find their seats for *Il Muto*
- Christine's lines as she leads Raoul to the roof "To the roof we'll be safe there!"
- The chaos that ensues upon the discovery of Piangi's body after *Don Juan Triumphant*

Regarding the London production, only a few of these scenes are literally marked in the scores as pre-taped, or pre-programmed on synthesisers. These include the overture, the Phantom and Christine's first descent to the lair featuring the title song, Red Death's lines and the background music until Raoul says "Madame for all our sakes …," and the second 'Notes Scene' in the manager's office.[170] Possibly, the remaining sequences are recorded in the London production, but they are not indicated in the scores. This cinematic element is an astonishing feature that separates the

---

[170] Lloyd Webber, Original *Phantom* Orchestral Score; (London, The Really Useful Group, 1988), (pp. 3), (p. 92 – p. 1), (p. 44– p33 and p. 50– p. 39), (p. 60 –p.1). Piano Rehearsal Edition; (p. II/1–22 and II/1–24), (p. II/2–10).

modern musical from the genre of opera. One may argue the validity of including pre-recorded sections within a stage production that traditionally is recognised as a live performance medium. However, the public today is conditioned to the fast pace of movies and television featuring the seamless presentation of action. Walsh observes Lloyd Webber has acknowledged that fact as people have been 'weaned' to records and Hollywood films, and they wish to see genres that incorporate both mediums. Walsh amusingly comments people have become insensible to the fact that music is a live performance skill produced by human beings, and alternatively view music as a product emanating from a loudspeaker; in response, Lloyd Webber has incorporated microphones, speakers, sound boards and synthesisers into his productions.[171] Is this practise different from the traditions of Classical musicians who composed according to the current vogue of their times? Walsh remarks that one may criticise these modern techniques, but as long as the technology is available, it will be used.[172] And why not? This reflects the genres and culture of contemporary times, and with *Phantom*, the result is extremely effective.

The Music

The music within *Phantom* also displays the theory of modernity; sharing elements related to Classical music tradition and popular music culture. Concentrating on the Classical element, the connections with Wagnerism continue throughout this production.

---

[171] Walsh, *Andrew Lloyd Webber*, p. 9.
[172] Ibid.

When we initially consider Wagner's music dramas, our attention automatically focuses on his principles of the *leitmotif*. As previously discussed, leitmotifs were intended to create a musical fabric that continued to develop, and thereby dramatic, emotional and visual associations were expanded as an opera progressed. However, there is a distinction between Wagner's concept of the leitmotif and the embryonic leitmotif principle already applied in previous operas by other composers. These early motifs are distinguishable in that they include a repetition of a portion from a number featured elsewhere in an opera, and/or they are apparent outside set arias or numbers; therefore, they act as reminiscence motifs.[173] Experiments with these motif techniques are apparent within Wagner's compositions of the 1840s as both of these motivic styles are evident. Within the production of *Phantom*, similar experiments with the reminiscent and the leitmotif concepts are recognisable.

The musical commences with a prologue set many years in the future; the opening scene features an auction held in the opera house that apparently is in receivership. An aged Raoul notices a music box in the shape of a monkey which had belonged to the Phantom, and is successful in purchasing it; this music box introduces the first motif, [Example 1.], and although we are not aware at this point, it is from the song "Masquerade." As Raoul comments upon his new acquisition, he sings a second motif that will represent the dominion of the Phantom within the opera house and the power he wields over the characters. [This will be called the "Power Motif," see example 2.] This motif will appear in the "Notes

---

[173] 'The Music Drama and its Antecedents', *The Wagner Compendium*, p. 79. Dr. Morris, Lecture handout.

Scenes" as the Phantom makes demands upon the management, when Buquet warns the managers of the Phantom, and when Madame Giry instructs Buquet to prudently hold his tongue. In summary, these would represent the use of reminiscent motifs.

Ex. 1   Masquerade Theme/music box

Ex. 2   Power Motif

However, we may also discern an embryonic form of Wagner's leitmotif concept with these two musical examples as apparently, they have developed from each other. [See example 3.] In addition, a section of the "Power Motif" will appear slightly transformed when used for a different theme [Example 4.] when Raoul proclaims his love to Christine on the roof, and is developed again within the Masquerade scene as Raoul and Christine become secretly engaged. This connection of the "Power Motif" with the song "Masquerade" is an ingenious subconscious reflection concerning the development of the drama; the Phantom's power is in reality an

158

illusion, a figurative mask concealing the fact he is a man and not a ghost. This connection could also symbolise the Phantom's desire to relinquish his power for the love of Christine as the music box plays the "Masquerade" theme for her in his lair; he is not her Angel of Music, nor a Phantom, but simply a man who desires to be loved. As confirmation of this observation, the Phantom sings the lyrics of "Masquerade" near the conclusion of the production accompanied by the music box, "Masquerade, paper faces on parade. Masquerade! Hide your face so the world will never find you...." The Phantom concludes the Masquerade reference by singing "Christine, I love you ..." with the same phrase Raoul used when professing his love to Christine on the roof. He has released Christine, relinquished all power and is forsaken, abandoned to the vengeance of the approaching mob. Apparently, these two motifs are not simply reminiscent themes, but also display the development of emotional and dramatic situations similar to the function of Wagner leitmotifs.

Ex. 3   Masquerade 'compressed' into the Power Theme

Ex. 4 Masquerade compared with Raoul's Theme.

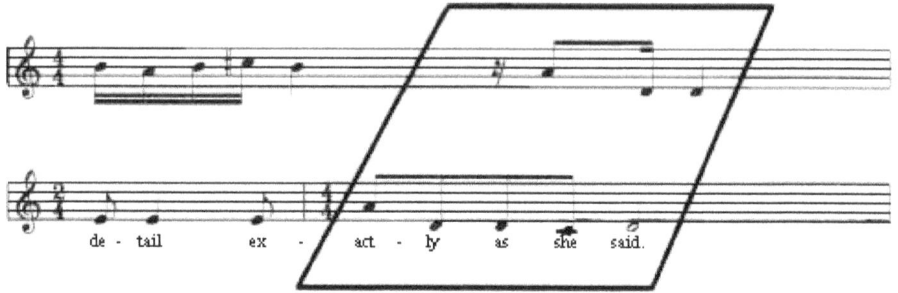

de - tail   ex   -   act - ly   as   she   said.

A similar motif that also portrays this dual characteristic of leitmotif and reminiscent theme may be termed the "Pity Motif." [Example 5.]   This theme is introduced after the horror of the Phantom's first unmasking has subsided and Christine returns his mask.   At first, the orchestra plays this theme while the characters are silent. As the plot develops Christine attempts to explain to Raoul during the Roof Sequence the story of the Phantom and her feelings towards this mysterious individual with the same theme, "Yet in his eyes, all the sadness of the world. Those pleading eyes that both threaten and adore." In the last scene, this theme is reintroduced as Christine sings, "This haunted face holds no horror for me now. It's in your soul that the true distortion lies."   Therefore, this melody appears as an 'emotional' introduction and plays an important role as the drama progresses; Christine attempts to address her feelings towards the Phantom, and ultimately portrays the resolution of her inner conflict.

Ex. 5 Pity Motif

Perhaps the most interesting reminiscent theme is the underlying motif of a rising fifth continually heard throughout the musical. [Example 6.] While it may not have a 'dual' function with the leitmotif concept as with the examples listed above, there is a coincidental link with Wagner. This rising fifth represents the Phantom's unseen, ominous presence within the opera house, and bears a striking resemblance to the rising fifth theme that introduces the character of the ill-fated Flying Dutchman. In addition, the five note chromatic theme first introduced in the overture is not unlike the chromatic passage heard in the *Flying Dutchman* overture. Both dramas address the issue of redemption achieved by a woman's love and therefore the connection between the two genres is appropriate. Intriguingly, Wagner considered the *Flying Dutchman* the turning point in his musical style, which corresponds to Walsh's observation that *Phantom* displays a marked development within Lloyd Webber's style as previously mentioned.

161

Ex. 6   Phantom Theme - rising fifth

K. II   "Phantom Shadow"

... perhaps we may
frighten away ...

... the ghost of so
many years ago
with a little ...

... illumination,
gentlemen?

Next, we will explore two themes, the "Angel of Music" theme, and the melody from the title song. These also have a reminiscent function, yet we may detect strong characteristics related to Wagner's ideal of motivic development. While the "Angel of Music" theme portrays Christine's naivety, it is modified melodically and rhythmically as her character develops. Before his death when Christine was young, her father promised to fulfil her childhood dream to send her the Angel of Music to complete her musical education. The Phantom discovers this may prove his only option to contact Christine, and assumes the role of the promised angel. As the musical proceeds, Christine visits her father's grave to release him from his promise and thereby free herself from the Phantom. The lilting 6/8 folksong melody of "Angel of Music" depicting Christine's naivety is transformed in "Wishing You Were Somehow Here Again" to an angular passage in 4/4 symbolising acceptance of the fact she can no longer live in dreams and past regrets. [Example 7.] The main title theme is modified in a similar fashion; for example, we hear this transfiguration when Raoul meets with Madame Giry who hesitantly informs him of everything she knows concerning the Phantom. Giry's theme features the driving, repeated quaver rhythm of the bass accompaniment of the title theme combined with a melodic variation

162

of the main melody. [Example 8.] This change in theme is confirmed by the verses sung by the angry mob as they descend into the cellars: "Track down this murderer he must be found, track down this animal who runs to ground! Too long he's preyed on us, but now we know, the Phantom of the Opera is here deep down below!" The mob repeats Giry's motif combined with the second half of the melodic phrase of the title song, which has been lengthened to include an echoing sequence on the words "Phantom of the Opera," thus depicting the cavernous depths of the cellars. This continual development of the title theme may symbolically represent the gradual decline of the Phantom's power as the Opéra populaire discovers he is human and not a ghost.

Ex. 7

"Angel of Music"

Some - how I know he's al - ways with me

he, the un - seen gen - ius. ——

From: "Wishing You Were Somehow Here Again"

No more me-mor - ies, no more si - lent tears, no more

gaz - in a - cross the wast - ed years. Help me say good - bye!

Ex. 8   Title Theme/ Giry's Theme

The romantic triangle between the Phantom, Christine and Raoul, and the interaction between these characters indicates a further development of Wagnerian concepts, also displaying a sophistication regarding key associations and the element of a 'subconscious' psychological progression.   Walsh has observed the key of D-flat signifies 'resonance' to Lloyd Webber; we denote this key is the tonic tonality of the musical, portraying the predominant ambience he wished to convey.   The revelation concerning the importance of this key is displayed through a gradual systemic technique.   Upon introducing Christine to his home in the cellars, the Phantom informs her that he has "brought her to this kingdom where all must pay homage to music," and adds she is there solely for the purpose of singing "his music."   He sings this passage accompanied by a whole tone chord progression [Example 9.], destined to assume an important role, though his words are cryptic for the present. Proceeding this unusual introduction, he sings "Music of the Night" in the key of C-sharp, (the enharmonic equivalent, and therefore the

164

same key of D-flat). This song concludes with a similar whole tone progression before resting on the tonic of C-sharp. The following morning, he assumes work on his composition featuring a variation of the whole tone chord accompaniment that he first sang to Christine. In Act II, scene 7 we recognise this whole tone material is the integral orchestral fabric of his opera *Don Juan Triumphant*, as the Phantom assumes the role of Don Juan and proposes to Christine, we are aware of a subconscious affiliation with "Music of the Night". The Phantom has deemed himself the personification of music; therefore, when he informed her she was to "sing for my music," he intended her to marry him. Perhaps this displays the Phantom's repressed emotions, he cannot state openly to Christine he loves her until the show is approaching the conclusion. He wishes her to take part in the 'opera' of his life, as symbolised in her participation in *Don Juan Triumphant*, hence, in contrast to the 'dark' five-flat key signature of D-flat major, he sings "Music of the Night" in the 'bright' enharmonic equivalent of C-sharp major featuring seven sharps. This may signify hope that his plan would succeed whereby Christine would save him from his wretchedness. Confirming this psychological connection, Walsh points out that the first version of "Music of the Night" was originally intended for *Aspects of Love* and was entitled "Married Man."[174]

---

[174]   Walsh, *Andrew Lloyd Webber*, p. 182.

Ex. 9   Whole Tone Theme

I have brought you to the seat of sweet mu - sic's throne,

to this king-dom where all must pay hom-age to mu - sic... — mus - ic... —

hrns.

harp

Ex. 10

Music of the Night

All I Ask of You

Music of the Night

All I Ask of You

166

is a counterpart of "Music of the Night" [Example 10*]; also, the introduction to "All I Ask of You" features the concluding chord progression from "Music of the Night". This parody between the courtship scenes shed light on the nature of the Phantom and Raoul's love for Christine. Ironically, when Raoul sings "Let daylight dry your tears" in the 'dark spectrum' of D-flat, it is night time; when the Phantom sings "turn your face from the garish light of day" while in the 'bright spectrum' of C-sharp, they are in the dark recesses of the caverns.   Notwithstanding his hope of winning Christine, the Phantom does not delude her concerning the nature of his existence in the cellars, while Raoul's affections appear misdirected, he does not take Christine's account concerning the Phantom seriously at first, and his words of love are tainted with chronological errors and the 'dark' nature of D-flat.   However, at the conclusion, Christine chooses Raoul; as they leave the cellars, the Phantom concludes the musical with the theme of "Music of the Night" in the key of D-flat, "It's over now, the Music of the Night." His dreams have been shattered, negating the 'hopeful' enharmonic key of C-sharp.

Obviously, the Phantom portrays similarities and parallels with contemporary Wagner culture. Lloyd Webber presents the Phantom as a musician who is ahead of his time by adopting the whole tone Debussy-styled harmony to display this musical advancement. In contrast with the Meyerbeer and Salieri pastiche scenes, the Phantom's music within *Don Juan Triumphant* is reminiscent of Wagner's progressive harmonies when compared with operas of his time. Similar to Wagner's ideals, the Phantom wishes to introduce a new concept of opera, elevating it to a new

---

* In the Hal Leonard piano/vocal edition, "Music of the Night" has been written in the key of D flat; however, according to the original score the key is in C sharp.

level in opposition to the opera managers, who prefer to pander to the masses. They wish to produce the established, standard repertoire as they state, "Nothing like the old operas, or the old scenery, the old singers, the old audience, and every seat sold!" Apparently, Lloyd Webber has retained Erik's preferences for *avant-garde* compositions as depicted in Leroux's novel.

Concerning the subject of Classical and mass culture associations within the score, we will examine briefly the nature of the 'cinematic' elements. Two prime examples of these features include the auction in the prologue and the scene in Christine's dressing room. [Examples 6 and 11.] These sections include dialogue passages underscored with an orchestral accompaniment; while this is not an original concept as it has existed with the German *melodram* of the 1700s, it bears a striking resemblance to a film score. These underscored sections prove advantageous as they bridge the varied expanse of complete spoken dialogue with the musical numbers or songs, thus eliminating the possibility of 'jolting' experiences encountered with sudden interruptions and instant plunges from dialogue to music. We may acknowledge this displays how the various polarities, i.e. Classical and mass culture techniques, work harmoniously to fashion a work of modernity.

Ex. 11

Similar to Wagner's cinematic scores featuring sound effects, for example Kundry's notated screams in *Parsifal* and the anvil music depicting Alberich's dwarves smelting metals in *Rhinegold*, Lloyd Webber also incorporates elaborate sound effects into the score of *Phantom*. One instance figures the disruption caused by the Phantom during a production of *Il Muto*, Carlotta, the prima donna, has ignored the Phantom's warnings and assumed the leading role, insulting Christine in the process by calling her a 'little toad'. In revenge, the Phantom using his skill of ventriloquism and magic, creates the illusion she has lost her voice as she croaks like a toad. The orchestra is instructed to 'go bezerk' as she loses her voice, thus displaying total chaos from the orchestra pit, the instructions read: "Round and round getting faster and faster. By about the fifth time the orchestra can play these notes in any time therefore sounding untidy. It is stopped by the manager's cue."[175] A particularly amusing example of cinematic sound effects include the notated 'tune-up' of the orchestra before the production of *Don Juan Triumphant*, the instruments are instructed to perform certain tasks in a manner similar to a graphic score as the conductor keeps time while invisible to the audience. Certain instruments are assigned a melody to 'practise' and are given unusual directions. The bassoonist is instructed to play the melody 'badly' and 'to squeak if possible'! The celeste is marked 'make it sound difficult'. The oboes and clarinets are instructed to sound the traditional 'A' for tuning and to 'play through their reeds'. The strings are assigned whole tone scales, pizzicato, and tremolo passages. The horns are to select some phrases from the next scene and to 'practise' them.[176] Incidentally, Lloyd Webber had obtained considerable experience with film music as he composed the score for the movie *The Odessa File.*

Apparently, unique sonorities were specially devised for the electronic synthesisers. During the Prologue, the auctioneer is accompanied by Synthesiser II that is marked 'auction', and as he says "Perhaps we may frighten away the ghost of so many years ago..." the Phantom's theme of a rising fifth is played by the synthesiser which reads 'Phantom Shadow'.[177] [Example 6.] The 'Phantom Shadow' sonority returns as his shadow materialises behind the backdrop during the production *Il Muto*.[178] In Act I, scene 3, Christine and Raoul recall their childhood, accompanied by the synthesiser marked 'dream'.[179]

---

[175] Original Score, (p. 234. p. 16.)
[176] Ibid. (p. 140, p. 1) to (p. 141, p. 2)
[177] Ibid. Prologue, (pp. 3–4)
[178] Ibid. (p. 242. p. 25)
[179] Ibid. (p. 79, p.1)

Other instructions are noted within the score that correspond with various special effects, for instance, when the Phantom shoots magical fireballs at Raoul, these actions are underscored in a similar fashion to the *melodram* technique observed earlier. Similar to Wagner's 'screams' for Kundry, Lloyd Webber notated the Phantom's stifled exclamation of "Oh, Christine!" concluding his passage "Fear can turn to love ..." after the first unmasking with note-heads marked by an 'x' indicating the words are to be spoken, but not to lose their halting, sob-like rhythm.[180]

This musical clearly portrays the concept of the modernity theory; there are many contrasts with Classical music, and the popular music/ mass entertainment culture similar to the ideology of Wagnerism, yet, these polemic elements work in harmony to establish this genre as a unique entity.

Phantom as an Example of the Modern Musical

Today, we may regard the modern musical an active example of Wagner's *Gesamtkunstwerk* ideology where all the arts would be combined in a uniformed manner. During the "Musical Theatre Renaissance" of the 1970s and 1980s, there was a gradual development towards the uniformed, 'official' production stage design. This method of production became evident when producer Cameron Mackintosh insisted that the standard of every touring production of *CATS* be the same as the original production.[181] From

---

[180] Ibid. (p. I/3–24.)
[181] 'The Phantom of the Opera', *The Musicals Collection* (EEC: Orbis Publishing Ltd., 1994), p. 25.

that time, all new musicals he produces such as *Miss Saigon* and *Les Misérables* feature the same sets and costumes for the various international productions, lending a unified set standard which establishes them with an 'official production' status. This is similar to Wagner's insistence that the *Ring Cycle* and *Parsifal* be produced solely at Bayreuth to ensure its continuity and maintain his original artistic signature. *Phantom* proves to be no exception; productions throughout the world are for the most part replicas of the original premiered in London. Apparently, this trend will continue as audiences familiar with the cinema relate to this method of presentation; perhaps the success of this method may be attributed to the fact one may attend a show which still maintains the composers'/producers' original intentions and artistic expressions. Lloyd Webber is adamant in maintaining his personal control over the development and production of his works, preferring to select people for his creative teams whom he believes share similar interests in his ideas for each musical at any given time. For instance, he chose Hal Prince to direct *Phantom* because Hal Prince wished to search for the deeper meaning within the drama, and like Lloyd Webber, desired to work on a romantic musical. Walsh states Prince was not elected to direct the production of *CATS* because he questioned the meaning and purpose of the plot, (or lack thereof), while Lloyd Webber simply wanted to develop a production that featured dancing and singing cats and wished the show to be accepted and enjoyed for its entertainment value.[182]

While we may argue this style propagates a 'static' genre that allows no space for the development of new production designs and

---

[182]   Walsh, *Andrew Lloyd Webber*, p.177.

personal artistic interpretation, there are variations evident within each production. Several of these changes are required due to the limitations encountered concerning the touring venues. In Tokyo, the stage was wider and shorter than those in England or America; Walsh comments that attending this production was similar to "watching a Cinerama movie shrunk to fit on television."[183] Other theatres do not have the requisite trap doors to accommodate the candles rising out of the lake, or Red Death's spectacular disappearance through the star-trap in the stage. To compensate, the candelabras appear from the wings, and Red Death must compromise his magical disappearance and simply exit the stage.

Changes to the score are apparently an ongoing process; observably the London production performing today contains many lyric changes not featured in the original London cast recording. The score originating from 1986 contains many new manuscript sheets at sections where these alterations occur. Perhaps these new additions were intended to 'refresh' material which may have become too familiar through the recording, thus encouraging 'arm-chair audiences' to attend a live production when and if possible. Of noticeable interest, a separate section of manuscript is included with the original score with the instructions it is to be included within the touring productions outside the London version. Other changes were possibly intended as improvements; for instance, the character of Piangi has received additional consideration in "Prima Donna", and corrections of grammatical errors such as the Phantom praising Christine in her dressing room are included. (The Phantom originally sang "Bravi, Bravi, Bravissimi," but this Italian phrase is plural, and

---

[183]   Ibid. f., p.206.

173

the intention was to praise Christine, therefore they modified it to "Brava, Brava, Bravissima," the singular feminine tense.)

A personal interpretation by the performers is acceptable in certain instances. Michael Crawford employs a 'dialogue to music' technique where he speaks/sings in moments of anger, e.g. at "The world showed no compassion to me!" in the recording. Mike Sterling also used this technique in the final Lair scene in the London production. The obvious disadvantage with this style, the melody is slightly obscured, and this could weaken the motivic reminiscent and leitmotif techniques if not heard properly. Performers may also ad-lib; Mike Sterling embellishes the scene where Christine, already released, returns onstage and hands the Phantom the ring. Sterling initially acts surprised, perhaps the Phantom assumes she has changed her mind, but then realises her intention was to return the ring, and he appears shattered. Although not indicated in the libretto, Sterling repeats the line "I love you ..." as she leaves with Raoul.

In summary, it is possible to envisage the modern musical as a form of the *Gesamtkunstwerk* principle. Adorno once stated the concept of a completely unified artwork would be successful if people could recognise all the elements that form its construction; arguably, this has been achieved with the modern musical. As an example of the modern day musical and Lloyd Webber's work, *The Phantom of the Opera* may truly be considered a composition of modernity comprising both Classical and mass culture elements in a harmonious fashion. By examining this musical in comparison to Wagner's works, and the aesthetics that distinguish them as works of modernity, it hopefully has been established that the modern musical from the 1970s and 1980s had evolved from traditional operatic categorization and entered a new echelon, a true "Musical Theatre Renaissance," particularly with the inclusion of cinematic techniques.

This neoteric development of the musical is manifested in the various conventions associated with production practises and audience attendance, transcending those experienced with opera, film, and popular culture. The modern musical has carved a unique niche in the cultural / entertainment industry. For instance, it is not confined to the duration of an opera season; a musical may run indefinitely and is therefore a 'living' genre — *Phantom* has been continually performed since October 1986. In addition, the modern musical is not held hostage by our contemporary society where consumers demand instant convenience and satisfaction as displayed with the "instant ennui syndrome" with cinema culture; the *zeitgeist* experienced is ephemeral as we eagerly await the next blockbuster, demonstrated by the customary previews before the feature film. Devoted fans of a successful musical from all factions of society will attend a production time and time again, and are prepared to travel to the capitals of the theatre world to view a production, not withstanding the expense involved. Thus, their enthusiastic loyalty contributes to the longevity of this 'living' genre— a phenomenon not generally perceived in the world of cinema.

Walsh states many critics are lacking in adequate training in music, or are insufficiently accomplished to understand the modern musical, bringing shame to journalism and a disservice to this new art form as they criticise the genre unjustly.[184] I suggest a positive perspective and attitude towards the modern musical may be

---

[184] Ibid. p. 10.

achieved if critics accept that it is a separate and 'new age genre' from Classical opera due to its cooperation with popular culture and the inclusion of unique cinematic elements.

❧ ◆ ☙

A Select Bibliography[*]

  ❧ Purcell's *Dido and Aeneas* (1689):
A Musical Exemplum for Young Gentlewomen

Dryden, John, trans. *Virgil's Aeneid*, Eliot, Charles W. ed. *The Harvard Classics*, Vol. 13. New York: P.F. Collier and Son Corp., 1963.

Price, Curtis, ed. *A Norton Critical Score, Henry Purcell, Dido and Aeneas, An Opera* New York: W.W. Norton and Company, 1986.

Scholes, Percy A., ed. *The Oxford Companion to Music.* Oxford: Oxford University Press, 1943.

  ❧ Hogarth, Handel, and 'The Levée' from 'The Rake's Progress':
A Satirical Portrait Worth a Thousand Words

Deutsch, Otto Erich. *Handel: a Documentary Biography.* New York: Da Capo Press, 1974.

---

[*] Website URLs were correct at time of composition. The author does not accept responsibility for inaccuracies if Webmasters have changed or moved sites.

Hogwood, Christopher. *Handel.* New York: Thames and Hudson Inc., 1984, 1988, 1995.

McCleave, Sarah. *Dance in Handel's Operas: The Collaboration with Marie Sallé,* PhD. University of London, King's College, 1993.

McWilliam, Neil. *Hogarth.* London: Studio Editions, 1993.

Shesgreen, Sean, ed. *Engravings by Hogarth; 101 Prints.* New York: Dover Publications Inc., 1973.

❧ The Symphonies of Beethoven: Historical and Philosophical Reflections through Music

Debussy, 'Monsieur Croche the Dilettante Hater,' Found in *Three Classics in the Aesthetic of Music.* New York: Dover Publications, 1962.

De Nora, Tia. 'Beethoven and the Construction of Genius.' *Musical Politics in Vienna, 1729–1803.* Berkeley: University of California Press, 1995.

The Great Composers: Beethoven. London: Marshall Cavendish Ltd., 1995.

Rosen, Charles. *The Classical Style, Haydn, Mozart, Beethoven.* London: Faber and Faber, 1971.

Solomon, Maynard. *Beethoven.* Schirmer Books, 1979.

Winter, Robert. 'The Ninth Symphony.' *Microsoft Multimedia Beethoven.* CDROM U.S.A.: Microsoft Corporation, 1991–1994.

🙖 Liszt, Goethe, the *Faust Symphony*, and the Symphonic Poem: 'The Word Must Become the Deed'

Barrett 'Batt', Oswald. 'Liszt the Traveller.' Plate 93, Scholes, . Percy A. ed. *The Oxford Companion to Music.* Oxford: Oxford University Press, 1942.

Einstein, Alfred. *Music in the Romantic Era.* London, J. M. Dent and Sons, Ltd.,1947.

'Faust', *Microsoft Multimedia Encyclopedia Encarta.* CDROM. U.S.A.: Microsoft Corporation, 1992–1994.

Goethe, Johann Wolfgang von. "Faust, Part I." W. Eliot, Charles, ed. *The Harvard Classics*, Vol 19. New York: P.F. Collier and Son Corporation, 1963.

Searle, H. Record notes, 'A Faust Symphony and Symphonic Poem, 'Orpheus'.' Hayes, Middlesex, England: E.M.I. Records Ltd., 1959.

Vazonyi, Nicholas. 'Liszt, Goethe, and the Faust Symphony.' *Journal of the American Liszt Society* 40 (1996).

Walker, Alan. *Franz Liszt; The Weimar Years, 1848–1861,* Vol II. New York: Alfred A. Knopf Inc., 1989.

Website;

Brians, Paul. Department of English, Washington State University, September 2000. Website; —
http://www.wsu.edu:8080/~brians/hum_303/faust.html

   ❧   Orientalism, Music, and Debussy:
       West Meets East

Einstein, Alfred. *Music in the Romantic Era.* U.S.A.: J.M. Dent and Sons, Ltd., 1947.

Said, Edward W. *Orientalism.* England: Pantheon Books, St. Ives plc., 1978.

Schmitz, Robert. *The Piano Works of Claude Debussy.* U.S.A.: Duell, Sloan and Pearce Inc., 1950.

Sorrel, Neil. *A Guide to the Gamelan.* London: Faber and Faber Ltd., 1990.

Vallas, Leon. O'Brien, Maire, trans. *The Theories of Claude Debussy — Musicien Français.* New York: Daver Publications, Inc., 1967.

Wilkins, Nigel, ed. and trans. *The Writings of Erik Satie.* London: Ernst Eulenburg Ltd., 1980.

❧ Andrew Lloyd Webber's *Phantom of the Opera*: An Example of the 'Musical Theatre Renaissance'

Forsyth, Frederick. *The Phantom of Manhattan.* Great Britain: Bantam Press, 1999.

Kay, Susan. *Phantom.* New York: Island Books, Dell Publishing, Delacorte Press, 1991, 1993.

Kempis, Thomas A. *The Imitation of Christ, Book I Chapter XXII.* Eliot, Charles, ed. *The Harvard Classics.* New York: P.F. Collier and Son Corp., 1963.

Leroux, Gaston. *The Phantom of the Opera.* United States: Dorset Press, 1988.

Lloyd Webber, Andrew. 'The Paris Opera House.' *Phantom Souvenir Programme.* London: Dewynters Plc., 1986, 1994.

Mackintosh, Cameron. 'The Phantom's Trail.' *Phantom Souvenir Programme.* London: Dewynters Plc., 1986, 1994.

Mage, Bryan. *Aspects of Wagner.* Oxford University Press: 1988.

Perry, George. *The Complete Phantom of the Opera.* New York: Henry Holt and Company Inc., 1988.

'The Phantom of the Opera.' *The Musicals Collection.* EEC: Orbis Publishing Ltd., 1994.

Programme note. *The Phantom of the Opera.* Theatreprint. Great Britain

Swain, Joseph P. *The Broadway Musical, A Critical and Musical Survey.* Oxford University Press, 1990.

Tambling, Jeremy ed. *A Night at the Opera, Media Representations of Opera.* London, John Libbey and Co., Ltd., 1994.

Walsh, Michael. *Andrew Lloyd Webber; His Life and Works* New York: Harry N. Adams Inc., 1997.

Websites;

'The Musical, Illusion — Backstage Interviews.' *The Phantom of the Opera, United States,* Website: Cameron Mackintosh and the Really Useful Group — http://www.thephantomoftheopera.com/musical/illusion/backstage.html

The Phantom Appreciation Website. 'Secrets of the Show' — http://phantom.simplenet.com/record.htm

A Select Index

186

196

෨◆෨